FINLAND IN EUROPE

Matti Klinge

Finland in Europe

OTAVA PUBLISHING COMPANY LTD.

Parts of very old rock paintings have been preserved on the lake shore rocks of the Finnish interior; most frequently they can only be seen from a boat. Rock paintings have been found in various parts of Finland and Russian Karelia. They may be four–five thousand years old.

Between east and west

Some ten thousand years ago, following the retreat of the continental ice-sheet, the first scattered settlements began to appear on the broad expanse of land, covered with lakes and forests, between the Gulf of Finland, the Gulf of Bothnia and Lake Ladoga. It is thought that the inhabitants of this area belonged racially and linguistically to the Finno-Ugrian group of peoples long before the Finns who gave their name to the country and its people migrated from the southern reaches of the Gulf of Finland to the southwestern part of the Finnish peninsula at the beginning of the Christian calendar. But there is a difference, thousands of years old, between the inland and coastal areas of this region; it is reflected in the way of life of the people and in their artifacts and is probably based on different racial and cultural traditions.

The important migration of peoples reached present Finland sometime prior to 3000 B.C. already; this migratory group which left behind combishly ornamented ceramic receptacles was apparently large, and its principal source of livelihood is presumed to have been sealing. Approximately between 1500 B.C. and 1000 A.D. contacts and migration took place essentially in the south whereby there was an influx into the present Finnish area of people, objects, terminology and other influences, the most significant of which was husbandry. Baltic influences came from the Estonian-Livonian region but also directly from the southernmost Lettish-Lithuanian area and subsequently the Western Slavic area, which again provided connections with the Black Sea and Mediterranean regions and later on with particularly

The hammer or boat-axe culture was a dominant Scandinavian cultural form in western Finland some four thousand years ago.

the Eastern Roman Empire. The expansion of the Swedish settlement extended to Finnish coastal regions perhaps from the 9th century to the 14th century. The internal migration continued while Finland was part of the Kingdom of Sweden until 1809 and even further, although Finland subsequently has been more a country of emigration than one of immigration. All migrations have brought along genes and cultural influences, and whereas the immigrants mostly have represented a higher cultural and technological standard, they have thus had a stronger effect on the structure of culture and society.

According to the newest large-scale research based on the hereditary transmission of blood groups, about three-quarters of the racial genic substance of the present Finnish people are of western and southern origin, and one quarter of eastern origin; the western element is strongest in the west and in the coastal region, to the effect that there is almost no difference to be noticed between the present Finnish-speaking and Swedish-speaking population of western Finland.

On the other hand, the linguistic structure of the modern nation shows that the eastern language has been stronger than the western and that a great many inhabitants of Germanic origin have adopted the various dialects of Finnish, with the apparent exception of the very latest arrivals from the west and their offspring. In respect of the language it must be emphasized, however, that although the (present) Finnish language forms a historical linguistic group together with Estonian and some Baltic minor languages and the languages of certain Russian inland tribes and peoples, as well as very remotely with Hungarian, the matter is different in consideration of other language grouping principles. The vocabulary of modern Finnish is largely of Germanic origin, and in view of their meaning, all abstract concepts, in particular, and the words relating to material objects and society conform as a result of historical and religious traditions etymologically to those of German and particularly Swedish.

The eastern expeditions of the Viking Age followed an important route which led in the shelter of the Finnish coastal archipelagos to the bayhead of the Gulf of Finland, to Lake Ladoga and from there, southwards along the waterways, as far as to Constantinople. The Vikings ruled in Novgorod in 862, in Kiev in 882 and, as early as 860, they had made their first attack on the capital of the eastern Roman Empire. According to runic stones many Swedes were still making journeys to Russia and Byzantium in the 10th and 11th centuries, some of them settling there. Inhabitants of the area now known as Finland certainly also participated in these expeditions, and Finnish and Baltic heathens continued their plundering raids to the east and the west even after the Scandinavian Viking expeditions had ended; the set of Sampo poems known from the Finnish national epic Kalevala can be presumed to relate to this tradition.

The maps published in the 16th century atlas under the name of Ptolemy reflect the old but vague concepts of the Mediterranean world about the northern parts of Europe. The Baltic is known, but its shape, coastlines and connections to the east were for long obscure.

SCHONLADIA NVOVA

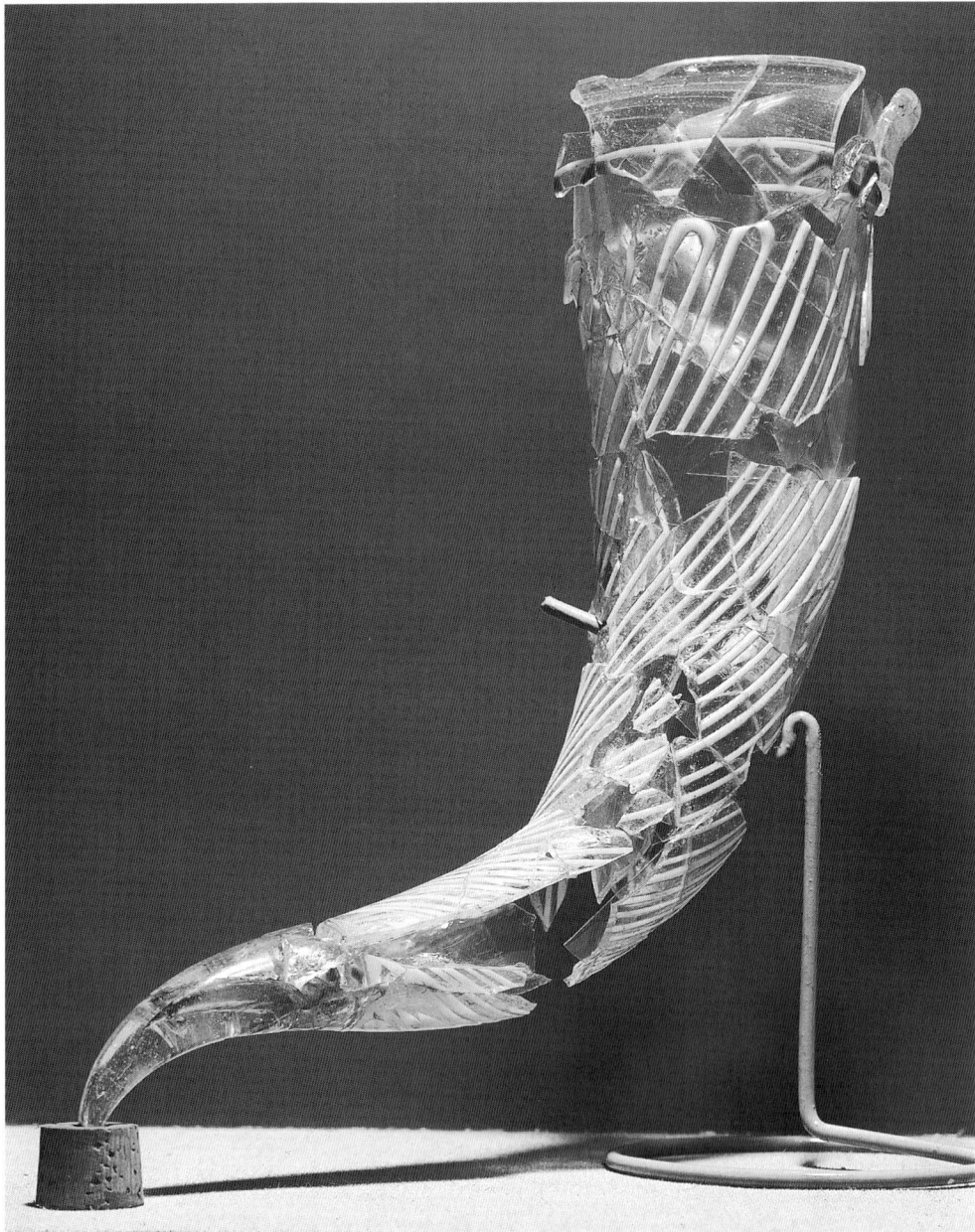

A Roman glass drinking horn found in southwest Finland from the fourth century is a reminder of the import of luxury articles.

Concepts of Finnish ancient history, language and characteristics started at the beginning of the 19th century to be profoundly influenced by the folk poetry collected on the periphery, and especially the Kalevala written by Lönnrot based on it. Some of the Kalevala heroic poetry seems more or less to reflect the 7th century Baltic aristocratic culture, in which piracy and probably slave trading played an important part. There the splendid swords of a manly cult seem to have been important, as is seen both in poems and grave finds.

Linked to this period of transition, the conversion of the Nordic countries to Christianity and their incorporation into the European ecclesiastical and emerging political organization, is the entry of Finland into documented history and the sphere of social conditions reflected therein.

At the dawn of the historical era the area that later became Finland was not yet a united whole. The main tribes, the Finns proper, the Tavastians and the Karelians differed from each other in many respects and were often hostile to each other. The Finns had connections to the west and south, the Karelians to the south-east; furthermore, the Åland Islands and part of Western Finland and the archipelago had belonged since an earlier period to the Central Swedish military and economic system. In the 11th century expeditions were made from Sweden and Denmark to western Finland. They followed the old eastern route of the Vikings and were evidently also undertaken in competition with Novgorod. The Kingdom of Sweden, now coming into being with the Uppsala-Sigtuna district at its centre, sought to stabilize old economic and cultural links with western Finland. Tradition has it that the first crusade (around 1155), led by King Eric and St. Henry, the Bishop of Uppsala, was undertaken to extend the area of the Swedish influence. This was accomplished through the establishment of the Finnish Missionary Diocese headed by St. Henry. Missionary work was conducted to-

18th century ryijy *wall rug, an example of Finland's very old textile culture, preserved as folk tradition. A "lion" rug from Myrskylä, in Uusimaa.*

wards Satakunda and along the Kokemäki River further also to Tavastia.

The fact that St. Henry was of English origin links the establishment of the Finnish Missionary Diocese with the general development in Scandinavia. The Catholic Church came to Finland from England after attempts to introduce it from northern Germany had failed. Although there are virtually no written sources describing Finnish history in the 12th century, the scant historical evidence that does exist, together with more plentiful archaeological findings, is sufficient to show that Christianity took permanent root in south-western Finland and that religious, economic and political links developed between this area and Svealand and east Götaland. At the same time Novgorod was taking an open interest in the people and trading places along the shores of the Gulf of Finland and Lake Ladoga. This area too was united by religious, economic and political interests.

The Danes and Germans were also interested in the coastal regions along the old eastern route. Sweden failed in its attempt to gain influence in western Estonia and it was the King of Denmark who conquered the western and northern parts of the country and established Tallin in 1219. At the same time the Teutonic Knights were attempting to push northwards and gained temporary hold of Estonia but it was soon re-taken by the Danes. Meanwhile the second crusade, from Sweden into Tavastia, had taken place under the leadership of Earl Birger. With Swe-

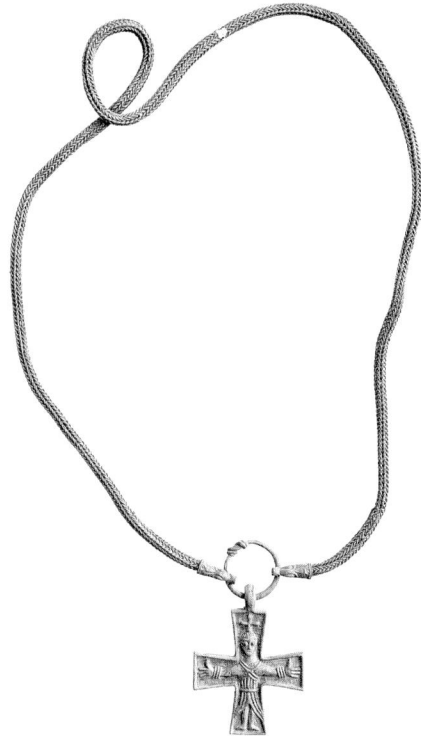

The cast two-sided silver crucifix from Maaria near Turku is from the 11th century, showing the early influence of Christianity before the organization of the Church became fixed. Influences and artefacts came from both east and west.

Like other European nations, the present Finnish nation has obtained its genes through constant visits from many directions, and Finns in turn have moved abroad at different times.

When the continental glacier of the Ice Age melted over 10 000 years ago, people came to the present Finnish areas along the fringe of the ice, apparently from the north, along the Norwegian coast, and from the south and the southeast. There had been human habitation of the Finnish area even before the Ice Age, over 100 000 years ago. These inhabitants were probably Neanderthals, and not the ancestors of the present Finns. Later inhabitants have come in several migratory waves, which have probably also spread to the present Northern Sweden and Northern Norway, and according to one theory to Estonia too.

Archaeological, linguistic and early historical evidence of migratory movements is difficult to interpret, and is therefore a constant subject of scientific debate. Evidence derived from artifacts and language tells us in any case of early links to the west (Sweden to-

In one of the best-known episodes of the Kalevala, the hero Lemminkäinen finds himself in the Kingdom of Death by the Tuonela river, and is rescued from it by mother love. The subject has been painted by R.W. Ekman in the 1860s and A. Gallen-Kallela at the end of the 1890s; in the 1860s Z. Topelius and F. Pacius touched on it in their musical play, and in the 1890s Jean Sibelius composed a symphonic poem about it.

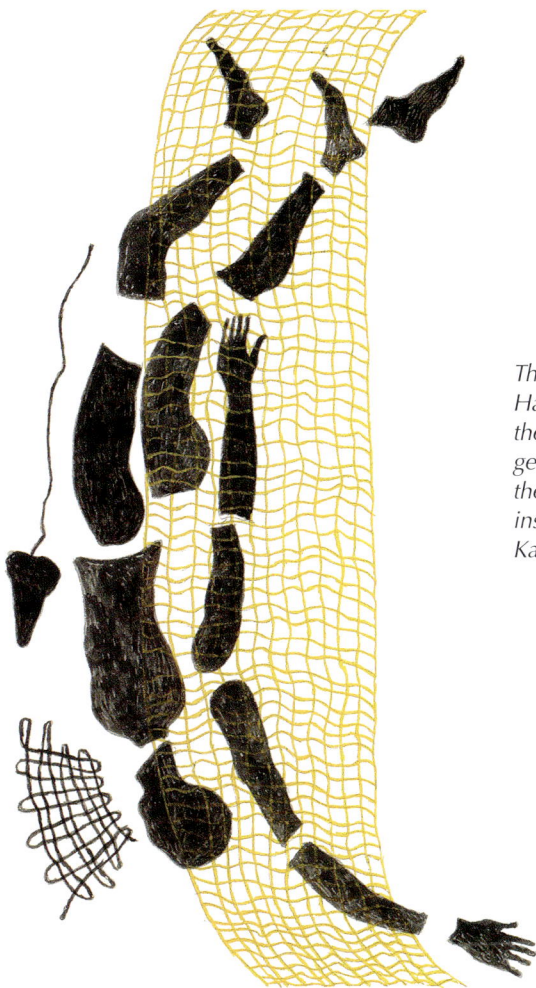

The well-known artist Hannu Väisänen and the Swedish sculptor Jörgen Hammar represent the most recent artists inspired by the Kalevala.

day), to the south (Poland and Lithuania today), to the southwest (Germany) and to the east-southeast, to the Volga area and further to the Altaic or Caucasian regions.

The structural and lexical basic structures of the Finnish language or languages (three main groups), and the Lappish and Karelian languages, connect Finnish to some Central Russian large and small ethnic groups, who were already living in these regions before the coming of the Slavs, and much more remotely to Hungarian and some Siberian languages. But constant contact with Germanic languages and other Indo-European languages, especially Latin, has affected Finnish sentence structure and, with the spread of culture, stylistic ideals. A considerable part of the older Finnish vocabulary, especially agricultural vocabulary, is of Baltic (Lettish-Lithuanian) origin, and a still larger part of the old agricultural vocabulary, along with a very considerable part of modern vocabulary, is of German origin, coming from Gothic, ancient Low German and ancient Swedish. The root forms of the main terms for values, colours, weapons and administration have come from these origins.

The development of modern culture from the 16th century Bible translations and from the 18th century culture to the modern Finnish of the educational system, politics and technology has of course been essentially enhanced by Latin-Germanic loan words – both direct and translated loans. In modern Finnish there are, as in other languages, very many new Greek-Latin words brought in with technology, often coming via English and French.

The Bible was already fundamentally translated into Finnish by the 1540s, and then completely in 1642. The Finnish language thus formed was strongly influenced by Latin, German and Swedish. The general culture of the Swedish kingdom affected structural, lexical and semantic aspects. The uniform legislation and court system, religion and church, as well as the administration and taxation of the whole realm created a semantic world that made Finnish and Swedish, at least up to the early 20th century, significantly the closest languages, in spite of structural and lexical differences.

When in 1809 Finland became a separate state, the Grand Duchy of Finland, deliberate efforts were made to shape Finnish into a uniform normal language. The Finns of the Turku area, who had given the name to the whole country and people, spoke a Finnish resembling the Estonian language phonetically and in other ways, and the inhabitants of the interior were divided into the language groups of the Häme and Savo historical provinces, with their different verb declensions, pronunciation and semantics. The influence of the Swedish language was felt strongly in Western Finland, that of Russian on the eastern border.

The Finnish press and literature, together with the education system increased the social and economic demand for Finnish, and in 1902 Finnish became the chief administrative language of Finland.

Genetic research in recent decades has revealed that Finns belong genetically to the general north European group, which today mainly speaks Germanic languages, except for some special genetic types observed in North-

A Finnish girl in St. Petersburg in the mid-19th century (Paysanne finnoise).

eastern Finland. Finns hardly differ genetically at all from the inhabitants of Central and Northern Sweden or of Norway, nor from the Estonians either. From this it may be concluded that in ancient times shifts of language occurred in such a way that a minority adopted the language of a majority, or that a majority adopted the language of a socially dominant minority. How these shifts came about is a subject of constant debate.

Swedish-speaking groups from what is Sweden today apparently moved to Finnish parts in the 5th and 8th centuries, to Western Finland (Satakunta), but these groups were already assimilated centuries ago. On the other hand, the Swedes who moved to Uusimaa and Ostrobothnia later, in the 12th and 14th centuries, preserved their language, because the dominant language of the integrated state of Sweden formed at that time was Swedish. Especially in the 18th and 19th centuries, the upper classes of Finland became entirely Swedish-speaking, (but also it is true often maintained practical contact with the language of the common people). For idealistic social reasons a great number of cultured people learned Finnish from the end of the 19th century, however, and then put their children into Finnish-speaking schools. This had a significant effect from the standpoint of national cohesion, and because the old heritage of culture was thus flexibly transferred to the Finnish language. By around the year 1910 at the latest Finnish had completely achieved the level of a European cultural language in every respect.

For some of the cultured Finns the Swedish language remained their principal language, however, at the same time as Swedish remained the language of some of the common people, and became a second national language. Its equal status was constitutionally secured in 1919 and 2000, although only less than six per cent of the total population still claim Swedish as their first language. The closeness and importance of Sweden also give the Swedish language considerable significance in Finland. Most of the Finnish population have some knowledge of Swedish.

Idealizing of the Kalevala and folk poetry led to the old rune singers being considered symbols of Finnishness: here the old Karelian woman Matjoi Plattonen is introduced to the King of Norway Haakon VII in 1928 in the Helsinki Kaivopuisto Park.

Finland's dozens of medieval granite and brick churches have generally lasted out till the present. Late medieval wall paintings still exist in many of them, for the Reformation's objection to pictures was not very strong in Finland.

An 11th century money find reveals a field of commercial connections. German, Anglo-Saxon and Byzantine money has been found in Finland and, as in all the Baltic area, abundant Arab coins.

den in control of Häme (Tavastia) and the establishment of a castle there, the coast of eastern Uusimaa (Nyland) began to be settled by groups of Swedish immigrants. The centre of the area was probably Porvoo (Borgå). The aim behind these measures was to provide support for attempts at expansion towards the east. While the Mongolians attacked Russia from the east, the Swedish "Prince" and his troops, whose numbers included bishops as well as Finns and Tavastians, pushed their way as far as the River Neva. It was here in 1240 that they were defeated by Alexander Nevski, the Prince of Novgorod, who two years later defeated the Germans in Estonia.

In the 13th century a loosely defined border dividing Swedish and Novgorod interests took shape. It extended from the River Kymi through eastern Tavastia to a point somewhere on the coast of the Gulf of Bothnia. The decisive struggle for possession of the eastern coast of the Gulf of Finland and inland Finland was fought at the end of the 13th and beginning of the 14th centuries. In 1293 Sweden embarked on the third crusade and founded the Wiborg fortress and city. During an expedition undertaken in 1300, the Swedes founded the Landskrona fortress on the banks of the River Neva, but this was destroyed by Novgorod. The long period of war came to an end with the Treaty of Pähkinäsaari (Schlüsselburg, now Petrokrepost) in 1323. It was here that, for the first time, the border between Sweden and Novgorod (later Russia) was agreed; not only a political border, it was also to divide two religions and two cultures. The people of Savo and western Karelia, whom destiny had placed to the west of the border, were to grow up, alongside the Tavastians and Finns, within the political and cultural sphere of the Kingdom of Sweden and under the Roman Catholic Church. The Swedish settlements in Uusimaa and along the coastal areas of Karelia, the Wiborg and

J

K

Savolai oder Neuschloss.
Nyschloss.
eine Vestung in der Provintz
Savolaxia in Finland. (Russisch seit 1714)

A. Plan des Schlosses Savolai oder Neuschloss
B C D die Thürne sind von den Russen gebauet
E F die Thurne sind von den Schweden gebauet
wie auch die Mauren von F bis C von E bis
B von E bis F

die Bresche ist geschossen worden von dem
Thurm E bis G In Prospect mit den accura-
ten grössen der Thürme von der seite E B D
H ist es sub Lit. J. der prospect von der seite
H L C M F Zeiget sich unter der Lit. K.

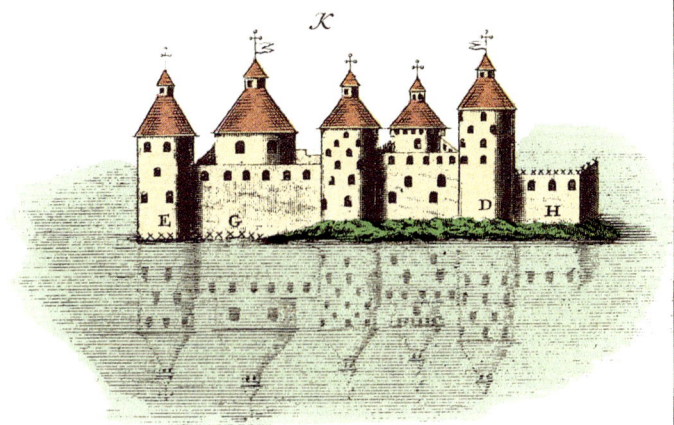

Olavinlinna Castle, built as a border fortress and a supporting fort for Viipuri at Kyrönsalmi on Lake Saimaa in 1475, was abandoned to Russia at the Peace of 1743; it now acted as a border fortress in the other direction. In the 19th century the district was no longer frontier country, and the castle was allowed to fall into decay, but after its 400th anniversary restoration was begun. Back in the 1910s and again from the 1960s it has been used as the stage for big summer opera festivals.

later the Olavinlinna fortresses, as well as the influence of trade and traders tied this area and its inhabitants to the West. Similarly, the Karelians, whom fate had placed east of the border, formed ever closer ties with Novgorod and the Orthodox Church. Later, the areas of North Karelia, Käkisalmi and the Karelian Isthmus were to be annexed to the Kingdom of Sweden and later still to the Finnish Grand Duchy. Thus the area, the people and the traditions that comprise modern Finland embrace Orthodox elements from east of the border as it was in the Middle Ages. How-

ever, the Finnish peninsula and its inhabitants were essentially linked to the emerging Swedish state and the Catholic Church. Indeed, the Karelians long referred to their western tribal brothers as "Swedes", a fact which demonstrates that, along the centuries, administrative and religious factors proved to be stronger than a common ancestry in the shaping of a nation's culture. The Finnish tribes, then, differed decisively from the Karelians and Estonians and joined the tribes of Sweden and the state growing up around them.

Ancient roads have been preserved in the man-made landscapes of Finland Proper. Per Olof Welin's photo of Uskela, a district where ancient memories bind its culture to the southern parts of the Baltic. The "Häme harbour" mentioned in chronicles may have been here.

PART OF THE KINGDOM OF SWEDEN

In the Middle Ages, as part of the Kingdom of Sweden, Finland had no special status which might have been reflected in such things as a separate administration, different laws or an addition to the King's title. From the outset the Kingdom was essentially a community which had grown up around the sea and the waterways (Lake Mälare) leading to the sea. The sea was to remain the most important means of transport and communications until the era of the railways. Cultural, commercial and administrative development in the peasant Kingdom of Sweden and in the areas to the east and west of the sea were largely dependent on influences from further south. From the beginning of the 13th century onwards the country experienced a change of decisive importance when the early influence of the English Church was replaced by a German merchant and city-centred culture. At the same time members of the nobility from the south coast of the Baltic and even further afield moved into the country mostly to fill military and legal positions. Estonia, the whole of which had come under the control of the Teutonic Knights in 1346 and whose capital had been predominantly German for some time, exerted a powerful influence throughout the Gulf of Finland area, as far as Turku and Stockholm. The influence of Sweden in the Middle Ages, on the other hand, can be seen clearly from the fact that only rarely did the families of the old local chieftains rise to the ranks of the nobility which had developed along with the system of castles and castle administration. On the

other hand, the Swedish peasant settlements in Uusimaa and Ostrobothnia grew up, side by side, with the Finnish, creating a unified western Finnish culture despite the maintenance of two separate languages. This culture can be said, perhaps, to have resembled that of eastern Sweden (Uppland – East Götaland) more than that of eastern Finland from which it differed in respect to traditions in agriculture, the family, artifacts and food.

An important feature of development in the 14th

The archaic granite castle of the powerful Fleming family at Parainen in the southern archipelago of Turku. Its location reveals the key importance and the need for defence of water traffic. The hall of Kuitia Castle.

Turku Castle is a mighty centre and expression of power that was extended over the centuries. It represented the authority of the Swedish king in the whole of Southwest Finland. The renaissance court of Duke John and his Polish wife Katarina Jagellonica in the 1560s was part of its period of splendour.

and 15th centuries was the way the Bishop's Seat in Turku, and their entire Church organization, established its position and thrived both spiritually and materially. As the ecclesiastical culture spread and took deeper root it tied Finland to the general sphere of European Christian culture. Gradually, stone churches, decorated with carvings and paintings, were built in all parts of inhabited Finland. The arrival in Finland of various monastic orders, including Dominicans, Franciscans, indigent orders and, later, the Order of St. Bridget, which took their place alongside the regular congregational clergy, strengthened the power of the Church. Journeys to the Papal curia in Avignon or Rome and, in particular, study trips to the famous universities on the continent, mainly to Paris, formed part of the universal ecclesiastical culture of the Middle Ages, and further advanced Finland's spiritual integration with Europe. Together with urban culture the influence of the church was felt specifically in the relatively densely populated areas of western Finland and was naturally weaker in those areas where, in addition to agriculture, life still revolved to a large extent round hunting

The Missale Aboense *is a great work printed for the Bishopric of Finland at Lubeck in 1488 – the magnificent first-born in the Finnish history of books.*

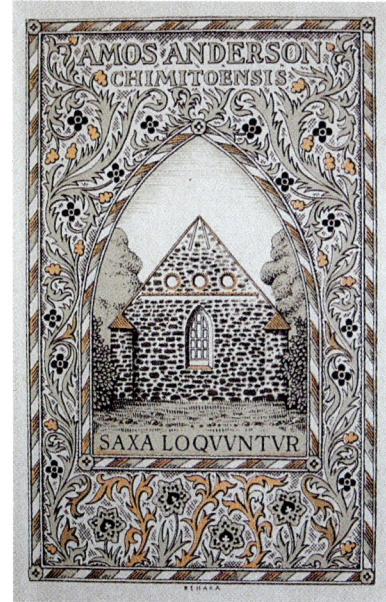

trips and other forms of livelihood requiring mobility. The most important centres from which the new influences spread were Turku, with its Bishop's seat and Cathedral, and Wiborg, both of which were the home of a number of important figures of medieval bourgeois society, particularly members of the artisan professions. The people of these towns had close contacts with the bourgeois culture of Tallin, Stockholm, Danzig and Lübeck, a culture which in the Middle Ages was largely German orientated.

At the centre of the Kingdom the name Eastland was sometimes applied to Finland (Proper) and the other areas beyond the sea, evidently in the same way that Northland began to be used as a general name for the provinces to the north of the centre. Eastland and Northland formed important and organic links with the centre formed around Svealand and Götaland. In the 1350's and once more in the 1440's a common Law of the Land was drawn up. It was compiled on the basis of the old provincial laws. Such laws had been unknown in Finland and Northland. In about 1350 a general Town Law was also drawn up. Thus Swedish law and a Scandinavian social system became established in Finland. They were to remain permanent national characteristics, features which distinguish the culture of the Finns from that of the Karelians and the Estonians. The right of representatives of the Finnish body of *lagman* (law-man = the country's highest magistrate) to participate in the election of the King was confirmed in 1362. This legal system, together with the four-estate representation (the nobility, the clergy, the burghers and the farmers) which had developed since the beginning of the 15th century, gave Finland indisputable and full political rights within the Kingdom of Sweden – unlike those countries which were defeated and annexed to the Kingdom later in the 16th and 17th centuries.

During the period of the Scandinavian (Kalmar) Union in the 15th and beginning of the 16th centuries, the influence of Denmark was felt in Finland too. Supporters of the Union and those opposed to it (they might better be described as opponents to each successive leader of the Union) met in open conflict, e.g. in the 1430's, the time of Engelbrekt Engelbrektsson and the 1470's, the period of Sten Sture the elder. Finland cannot be said to have formed a political entity or unit where this issue was concerned, but in practice it did function as an area of economic support, securing

The Finnish 15th century translation of the Swedish kingdom's general law of the land of 1442 begins with a description of the kingdom's appearance and the significance of the forests as boundaries.

Olaus Magnus' book, printed in Venice, stressed the fact, exciting to southern Europeans, that the sea and inland waters freeze in the northern winter, and that war can be waged and goods can easily be transported on the ice.

There were not only ice, winds, inland waters and ability to make war in the North, but also considerable grain harvests could be obtained by applying a special technique. There the forest is burned and the ash yields two or three excellent harvests, after which the farmer must move on to a new location. But there were abundant uninhabited woods in Finland in the 16th century and still much later.

power for Sten Sture for example. If it is possible to talk of nationalistic feelings at that time, in Finland too they were directed against the Danes.

The Pähkinäsaari Treaty of 1323 did not put an end to the question of the Swedish Kingdom's eastern border. Its southern reaches, it is true, were clearly defined and placed the districts of Jääski and Äyräpää on the Karelian Isthmus in Swedish territory, but the third area mentioned by name in the Treaty, Savo, because of the nature of its settlements and the forms of livelihood practised here, was not nearly so well defined. A semi-nomadic way of life and slash-and-burn agriculture, which meant the constant clearing of new land for cultivation, led to a complex system of ownership and property rights. The border ran northwards from the Karelian Isthmus to the sea, and it seems evident that there was a vast joint area of Swedish-Novgorodian dominance in the north where Swedish rights reached a borderline extending eastwards from the Karelian Isthmus to the Arctic Ocean, whereas Russian rights reached a borderline extending westwards from the Karelian Isthmus to Central Ostrobothnia and the Gulf of Bothnia and partly into the territory of present Sweden. Until still much later, the major part of Lapland formed a common taxation area of two or even three powers. As permanent settlement and farming spread to this joint area of usufruct or common taxation, conflicts arose over the borderline, and settlement became a form of land seizure. The Savo settlements spread out towards the east and, in the mid 1470's, the Lord of the Wiborg fortress, Erik Axelson Tott, built the Olavinlinna fortress on the border to provide support for expansion. The influence of Karelia-Novgorod was gradually pushed back from the coast of the Gulf of Bothnia. At all events, the districts of Pohjanmaa (Ostrobothnia) and Länsipohja (Westrobothnia) were deemed part of the Kingdom of Sweden in 1346 when the border between the Uppsala and Turku diocese was fixed as running between the River Kemi and the River Kaakama. Thus, by virtue of its expanding settlements, Sweden gained considerable areas to the east of the border as it was defined in the Treaty of Pähkinäsaari, a fact which led to continuous border conflicts. Sweden ignored the continuous demands of Novgorod that it should mark out its border in the terrain. When the border was eventually re-drawn at the Peace Treaty of Täyssinä (1595), it more or less followed the eastern limits to the Savo settlements, a border which had in fact been established in practice much earlier and which, by continuing to the Arctic Sea, also confirmed Swedish (and Danish) supremacy in Lapland.

THE BIRTH OF THE CENTRALIZED STATE

The collapse of the Scandinavian Union and the reign of Gustavus I Vasa (1523–1560) represented an important turning point in the history of the Swedish state and especially of its eastern territories.

Separation from Denmark and Norway on the one hand, and the Reformation, with its financial exploitation of the Church, on the other, led to Sweden's cultural isolation from the rest of Europe, with which it had become united in the international atmosphere of the 15th century. The trend to a more provincial culture, following the general principles of the Reformation, meant the appearance in Sweden of literature in both languages of the state, with the Bible translated into Swedish and (most of it) into Finnish. Other ecclesiastical and legal works also appeared in both languages. In translating such works into Finnish, Michael Agricola, rector of the Cathedral school in Turku, who had studied under Luther and Melanchton at Wittenberg and would eventually become Bishop of Turku, laid the basis for a Finnish literature. Following the Reformation, with Gustavus Vasa's expropriation of church property, there was little support for advances in the field of culture. The state profited considerably from the "nationalization" of the Church. In the Kingdom now separated from Denmark, Finland held a position of real importance, a fact reflected in the role played by members of the Finnish nobility in state administration and the army in the 16th century.

During the reign of Gustavus Vasa the country's economic structure underwent a decisive change with taxation and financial administration, previously

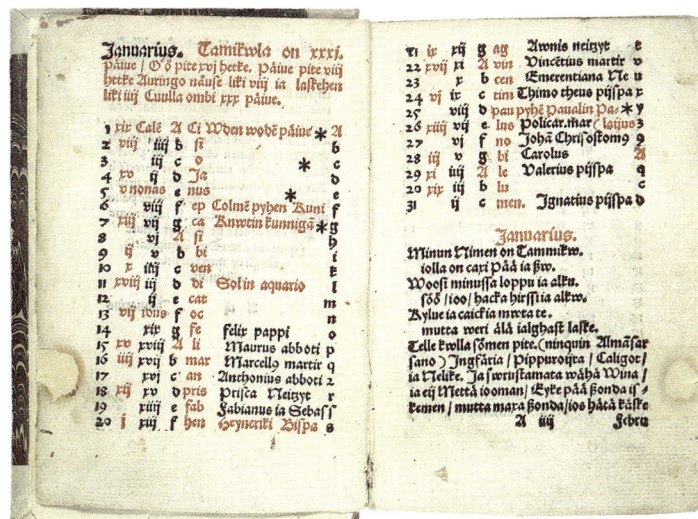

An extract from the calendar section of Agricola's Prayer Book: January. According to the calendar one should eat ginger, pepper and cloves in January. One should also drink only a little spirits and no honey at all. When letting blood the main artery should not be touched, but only, in extreme cases, the "liver vein". Agricola thus taught the clergy the lore of old medical textbooks; he refers to many antique and medieval authorities.

Michael Agricola was one of the young Finnish teachers and clergymen in the kingdom of Sweden who were able to study as formerly at universities in Continental Europe. The reputation of Luther and Melanchthon made Wittenberg an important intellectual centre as early as the 1520s. Agricola studied there from c. 1535–1539, and then returned as a magister to tasks in his own bishopric of Turku, although Melanchthon had recommended him as a teacher at the University of Uppsala, which had fallen into decay. Agricola first became head of the Turku school, until he was appointed assistant bishop of Turku in 1548, and Bishop of Turku in 1554. The bishopric of Turku was, it is true, divided into two at that time, and a new bishopric was established in Viipuri. Agricola himself had studied at the Viipuri school, and seems to have grown up in the German and the Finnish-Russian border tradition of the city. With his talent for languages he appears to have known Russian: he died on his return from a diplomatic mission to Moscow in 1557. He was still under fifty then.

Agricola's predecessor was still an ordained Catholic bishop and appointed by the Pope. Although Agricola was "only" appointed by King Gustavus I Vasa, he emphasized continuity by holding the traditional bishop's mass in Turku Cathedral. For the king of Sweden-Finland, a very important part of the change in the form of religion was the confiscation of the Church's great wealth, and the leaders of the Church had to fight against this and the accompanying vandalism in Sweden, the destruction of Catholic paintings.

Michael Agricola's most significant contribution is his extensive activity in the Finnish written language, which includes not only a spelling book and Luther's catechism, but also the translation into Finnish of the whole of the New Testament and a large part of the Old Testament. In addition he put together a Prayer Book (1544) of over 400 pages, partly in encyclopedic form, revealing the great power of the old Catholic tradition and thus the considerable moderation of Agricola's reformatory work.

Agricola had already begun his translation of the New Testament in Wittenberg, while later works

Among the essential themes of Finnish historical painting is the scene in which the Bishop of Turku and Reformationist of Finland, Michael Agricola, delivers the Finnish translation of the New Testament to King Gustav I Vasa. Actually the relations between the King and the Bishop were strained, since the Bishop was trying to oppose the King's ruthless confiscation of Church property. In a sense Agricola protested by holding a grand Catholic-toned Bishop's Mass in Turku Cathedral. The painting is one of Albert Edelfelt's lessknown works.

were performed in Turku in co-operation with students; all the books were printed in Stockholm.

Agricola's extensive early translation work raised him to the front rank of European translators of the Bible. Luther published the Bible in German in 1534, Olaus Petri in Swedish in 1541 – and Agricola's main works appeared as early as the 1540s. The New Testament was published in Finnish in 1548, only some twenty years after the Danish and Swedish translations, but Agricola did not have any previous Finnish-language writings as a starting-point. The Bible was translated into Polish a little later,

and it also appeared in Low German, and also perhaps in Lettish. Everywhere in the Baltic regions religious writing in the 16th century established the written language; everywhere the structure and vocabulary was also strongly influenced by Latin and German.

Not all the new written languages of the 16th century remained alive – neither for example Low German nor Lettish – writings in the latter disappeared completely. In the early 17th century further notable religious works appeared, the Postilla of Bishop Ericus Eric and in particular a complete, revised translation

of the Bible in 1642. But then the volume of Finnish writings rapidly diminished, as Swedish gained ground as the educated language and ever more widely as the language of everyday use in Finland. In the 18th century only one significant Finnish work appeared, Bishop D. Juslenius' Finnish-Swedish-Latin dictionary – extensive though it was – in 1745. In the latter part of the century antiquarians became interested in the Finnish language and folklore, but only a few religious writings were published in Finnish.

The situation changed rapidly when, in 1809, Finland became a separate political and governmental entity, and gradually a national idea – the fatherland. The Finnish language was then understood from the start to be important both symbolically and practically, and it began to be modernized.

Jesusen Cherstusen Vs=
colisten / pyhein ia Jumalallisten
Somalaisten / Hemalaisten / Pohialais=
sten / ia Carialaisten etc. Papeille / Sarna=
ille / ia caiken ychteitzen Seurakunnan / eli
Canssan / sen Christusen kihlattun fraa=
wan / caunin Morsiamen / puchtan Nei=
itzon / ia Taiualisen Trotingin / Mine Mi=
chael Olaui Agricola / Jumalan epckeluo=
toyn paluelia / henen pyhen Poians Eu=
angeliumisa / toyuotan Armon /
rauhan / laupiudhen / ia Juma=
lan teydhelisen Tundemisen
Jesuses Christuses mei=
den harrasanna / hian
caikisen ilon ia Ee=
lemen cansa
Amen.

Rucouskiran Esipuhe.

*In the 1540s Luther's pupil, Magister Michael Agri-
cola, who later became Bishop of Turku, translated
and edited a large quantity of writings into Finnish,
including the New Testament and much of the Old
Testament, together with ecclesiastical manuals for the
use of the clergy. The most significant of them is the
thick and encyclopedically diverse* Prayer Book from
the Bible, *which may be considered in its humanist
erudition the best utterance in the whole Swedish
realm in the 16th century.*

based on a system of castle *fiefs,* now the direct responsibility of the centralized state. The financial difficulties of the Crown, which led to the almost complete
confiscation of Church property, was also behind the
proclamation of 1542 claiming the uninhabited wilds
of Finland as Crown property. This paved the way for
extensive state-controlled territorial expansion, particularly in Savo where settlements built around the
method of slash-and-burn agriculture spread hundreds of kilometres to the north and north-west.

Throughout the 16th century, right up until the
Peace Treaty of Stolbova in 1617, Sweden's political
relations with Russia played a central part in the country's affairs. Behind this was not only dissatisfaction
with the border as it was defined at Pähkinäsaari but
also changes within Russia, the Baltic and Poland. The
war with Russia (1555–57) ended with neither side
having achieved a clear victory. With the collapse of
the Teutonic Knights in 1561, Tallin allied itself with
Sweden, but throughout the 1570's fierce battles were
fought with Russia both in Estonia and in Finland.
Swedish victories between 1580 and 1581, particularly those at Käkisalmi and Narva, led to the addition of
"Grand Duke" of Finland, Karelia, Ingria and a fifth
part of Vatja (Käkisalmi) to King John III's title. These
successes were due in part to the fact that Russia was
being harassed by Poland at the same time.

With his marriage to Catherine Jagellonica in
1563, John III had already strengthened Sweden's ties
with Poland. The marriage produced a son, Sigis-

A powerful military man of the 16th century, Admiral
Claes Christer's son Horn, as seen in the 1920s (T. Vikstedt).
The figure could also represent King Gustavus Vasa or the great
Marshal of Finland, Claes Fleming.

The Finnish coat-of-arms dates back to the time of King John III; the flag for funeral processions bears the letters I. R. - Johannes Rex. The coat-of-arms and the heraldic status of a Grand Duchy stem from the expansion of the Swedish kingdom to the east, when the need of the still quite young Vasa royal family to emphasize their position vis-à-vis Russia and Poland led to the addition of the new title to the royal titles. The message of the coat-of-arms is the opposition of two different kinds of sword; the scimitar might have referred originally to the Turks, but it was soon understood as a reference to the Russians.

mund, who became king of both Sweden and Poland.

In 1593 the clergy and also the other estates convened in Uppsala for a kind of parliamentary session at which Lutheranism was finally and definitely approved as the one and only established state religion. The Kingdom assumed from then on also features of a clerical state since the duties of the clergy were very comprehensive in the extensive provinces until the late 19th century; both the spiritual and educational and to a great extent also the economical and administrative leadership was mainly entrusted to the vicars. The clergy had already earlier constituted an estate of the realm, and in the Lutheran world, where clergymen lead a married life, the clergy became a hereditary estate similar to the nobility.

A civil war broke out later when Sigismund's uncle, Charles, the Duke of Södermanland, took up the cause of Protestantism and the centralized state in opposition to Sigismund who was supported by the Catholics and the higher nobility and who favoured a more old-fashioned type of decentralized state controlled by the latter. The Finnish Governor, Klaus Fleming, and most of the Finnish nobility supported the King in this dispute and were later to pay for this when the Duke won the war and became King Charles IX. In what is known as the Club (i.e. cudgel) War (1596–97), Charles was supported by the peasants of Ostrobothnia, Tavastia and Savo, who were discontented with the deterioration in social

A 16th century "perfume button", of gold, enamel and red stones, found in a field at Liuksiala, Kangasala, the manor of Karin Månsdotter, who was raised from lowly estate to become the queen of Erik XIV. Some fragrant substance was kept in the perfume button for the pleasure of the bearer and as a mark of social standing.

conditions and therefore rose up in rebellion. The rebellion, however, was put down by Klaus Fleming.

During the reign of Gustavus II Adolphus, son of Charles IX, war with Russia broke out once more with the states bordering on Russia attempting to take advantage of the country's internal disorder. During this war, which ended in 1617, Sweden annexed Ingria and the province of Käkisalmi, areas which it had temporarily held earlier. This left Russia completely cut off from the Baltic Sea.

The 16th century was characterized by attempts to strengthen the position of the Crown and to centralize state administration. So succesfully did Gustavus Vasa augment his position that in 1544 the system of elected kings was replaced with an hereditary monarchy. The centralization of tax collection and state finances made for considerable conformity, a development which was further strengthened by the transference to the state of the power and property of the Church. The struggle for power which followed when Gustavus Vasa bestowed Dukedoms on his sons (John was given the Duchy of Finland, i.e. the south-western part of the country, where, for a short period, he held what was for the times a magnificent Renaissance court in the Turku Castle) held back attempts at centralization. A struggle for power between the King and members of the higher nobility as well as a peasant rebellion brought about by the burden of a new administration and war machinery were common features in Europe at this time. As the Crown grew in

In the 17th century the elite of the Swedish realm were concentrated in Stockholm, which had finally become the capital, but nevertheless a couple of baroque castles were built in Finland. Louhisaari, belonging to the old Fleming family, came into the possession of the Mannerheim family, representing a new aristocratic stratum, in the 19th century; in 1865 Gustaf Mannerheim, later to become Marshal of Finland, was born there.

strength it attempted to turn the nobility, which was a more or less independent local gentry, into a body of civil servants and military officials. The execution of many of Sigismund's followers went a long way towards breaking the power of the nobility.

On the other hand, the continuous wars tended to stress the significance of the nobility, and by rewarding successful military leaders with prizes of land a kind of post-feudal situation was brought about. The change in the position of the nobility can be seen from the fact that, whereas in the latter part of the 16th century a number of Finland's leading families, including the Flemings and the Horns, had palatial mansions built, in the 17th century, with the exception of the Fleming family's Louhisaari and the Creutz' Sarvilahti, such extravagant family manors were not built at all in Finland. The powerful figures of the country tended to build their manors and palaces in or around Stockholm.

THE GREAT POWER

From the reign of Gustavus II Adolphus onwards, a characteristic feature of Sweden's period as a great power was the fact that, at first the Baltic countries, then Poland and finally Germany took the place of Russia as objects of Sweden's military and political ambitions. The wars in Germany were fought mainly with native Swedish manpower and this placed a considerable strain on the country's economy and population. This period of military activity, together with involvement in the wars on the continent, enhanced the position of the military leaders, that is to say the nobility. The Regency governments and the favourable attitudes of Queen Christina increased still further the prestige of the nobility. Many of those areas whose taxes were distributed as rewards for military achievements in the form of *fiefs* were located in Ostrobothnia and Karelia.

Another development during this period was the increasing importance attached to the position of Stockholm. With Stockholm the final home of central administration and with the Diet firmly rooted there through the erection of the first parliament building, the House of Nobility, the town exerted an influence on all parts of the Kingdom. Stockholm's position was also strengthened by a mercantile economic policy, one expression of which was the banning of foreign trade in towns along the Gulf of Finland and Gulf of Bothnia in favour of the capital. Thus the country's period as a great power saw the creation of a firmer administrative unity, a development that was felt in all walks of life.

During this period the main centres of population and the economic hub of the Kingdom of Sweden were situated around the waterways along the line Gothenburg–Stockholm–Turku–Tallin–Wiborg. At the beginning of the 17th century the emphasis was further to the east than it would be later, as

The whole Bible was published in Finnish in 1642. It was a splendid, large-sized, illustrated edition, with a picture of the young ruler of the kingdom, Christina, at the beginning. The only daughter of Gustavus II Adolphus "the Great" was then still a minor, and did not herself begin to rule until two years later. During her time, in 1640, a University of Finland was founded (today Helsinki University). It was during her reign that the general European Peace of Westphalia, victorious to Sweden, was concluded in 1648; this period marked a political and spiritual Europeanization. Christina herself became a Catholic, gave up the throne and lived most of the rest of her life in Rome. The picture shows all the coats-of-arms of the Swedish provinces; to the right of the main coat-of-arms, the coat-of-arms of "the Grand Duchy of Finland", still valid today. The status of the Grand Duchy was purely heraldic, and did not signify separate administration.

IDIBVS · IVLIIS · A · D · MDCXL

The inauguration prosession of the Royal Turku Academy in Turku, 1640. The original painting by Albert Edelfelt was destroyed in the heavy bombing of Helsinki in February 1944.

is indicated by the fact that the two universities established after that of Upsala were situated in Tartu (1632) and Turku (1640). Income received from Estonia and Lithuania was of considerable importance to the Kingdom. The composition of the ruling class was also altered with the intake of nobility from the Baltic countries. During the 1630's, with the war being waged for the most part in the south, the southern reaches of the Kingdom gained in impor-

tance and the inclusion in the realm of wealthy provinces seized from Denmark in 1658 meant that the country's centre of gravity shifted further west and further south. But it was not until the 18th century that Finland became a more peripheral region within the Kingdom. This was due, on the one hand, to the powerful growth of Gothenburg and trade with the west, and on the other, and this was more important, to Russian expansion westwards since the time of Peter the Great.

The establishment of a university (1640) and a Court of Appeals (1623) in Turku, the publication in Finnish of the complete Bible (1642) and the appearance of several new towns gives some indication of developments in Finland in the 17th century, a

Five Lutheran state universities were established in the Swedish kingdom in the 17th century. There had, it is true, been a small Catholic university in Uppsala before the Reformation, but it had ceased to function. In the same way there had been a university dating from the 15th century in Greifswald, Pomerania, but that had also to be revived after the destruction of the Thirty Years War, when Pomerania was annexed by Sweden. Completely new universities were founded at Tartu (Dorpat) in 1632 and Turku (Åbo) in 1640 during the eras of Gustavus II Adolphus, Queen Christina and Oxenstierna, and the University of Lund at the end of the century. The significance of the universities mainly corresponded to the field of the Courts of Appeal, but they were national and drew students from various parts. In those bishoprics where there was no university, semi-academic gymnasiums (secondary schools) were established; one of these was at Viborg, later moved to Porvoo when Viborg was lost to Russia. Turku University was transferred to Helsinki later (1828), also for political reasons.

There was no university in Stockholm, the capital. Three im-

Under the direction of professors of history, philosophy and rhetoric, thousands of small master-of-arts dissertations appeared in the University of Finland, most of them dealing with moral issues. Some of these were written by the professors themselves, and the students defended them publicly. One of them was this dissertation De amicitia. Some were written by students, such as De quatuor generibus mulierum – The Four Types of Women. The professors also wrote separate books; for example Achrelius on the writing of letters. All this promoted the implanting of mid-European Renaissance humanism in Finland.

Emperor Alexander I doubled the revenues of the University of Finland. Later the university was transferred from Turku to Helsinki, built to be the capital of the Grand Duchy, and was given the name of "Imperial Alexander's University". The light of the new age shines behind the university building, and a muse representing Finland conveys thanks to the ruler for culture.

portant academies were founded there in the 18th century, the Academy of Science for the natural sciences, the Academy of History, Literature and Antiquities for the humanities, and finally the Swedish Academy.

The Finnish university in Turku was small and modest; most of its students became clergymen. But the university was nevertheless very important in forming an intellectual class and implanting the written culture and knowledge of languages. Around the middle of the 18th century it was strongly utilitarian and physiocratic, but at the end of the century it became a stronghold of the German-inspired Neo-Humanism.

When the Grand Duchy of Finland was formed in 1809, the University was at once given the vital task of educating the new state's civil service and creating the national identity. Emperor Alexander I, after whom it was later entitled "the Emperor Alexander's University of Finland", favoured the university, first in Turku then in Helsinki, from the outset; it was given, considering the conditions of the time, splendid new buildings: main buildings, observatories, and

in Helsinki a beautiful large library, the Botanical Gardens, clinics and later much more.

The stressing of moral education for civil servants and the shaping of the idealistic concept of the nation gradually resulted in a high-level civil service and a well-functioning administration in Finland in the latter half of the 19th century. A vital factor was the idealistic concept of the people and the nation formed at the University and crucially supported by student youth. University teachers, the poet Runeberg, the discoverer of folk poetry Lönnrot, the social and cultural philosopher Snellman, the journalist and historian Topelius, the founder of the arts Fr. Cygnaeus and the founder of nationalistic history Yrjö Koskinen shaped the vital cultural content of Finland, the *Lehrgemeinschaft*, and taught it to students and the whole nation.

Students in the student unions, choirs and joint literary projects trained to become masters of verbal and written presentation and presenters of the idealistic message, at the same time as they prepared to take their part in the idealistic societies and economic

1897

PÄÄSYLIPPU

PROMOTSIOONI-JUHLAAN

YLIOPISTON JUHLASALISSA

MAANANTAINA TOUKOKUUN 31 p:nä 1897

klo 11 a. p.

Oikeanpuoleinen ovi.

Conferment of degree ceremonies of the Faculty of Philosophy have always included stylish printed products with variations of the symbols of Apollo's lyre, the laurel wreath, the torch of culture and Minerva's owl. The emblems of the Master of Philosophy have since the conferment of degrees in 1643 been the wreath and the ring; the doctor's emblems are the pleated silk hat and the sword. A lyre circled by a wreath is the symbol both in the ring and the cockade of the doctor's hat.

projects of their future regions of activity. The later great idealistic and also the central economic organizations of Finland have followed the university model. Just as there was a joint Student Union and unions according to provinces (*nationes*) in the University, there was a national and district organization in idealistic societies, parties, banks, etc.

By means of an extensive national subscription in 1870 the Student Union obtained its own building in Helsinki, known today as the Old Student House, in the heart of the city. Later the Helsinki University Student Union became very wealthy and influential; via leading positions in it very many have gone on to become leaders in politics and other fields. The Student Union and the University are strikingly present in the centre of the capital, firmly set alongside other state, local authority and business buildings and functions. This has been and is of great symbolic, practical and educational importance. The Finnish academic tradition has not been built on the small town or campus tradition, but according to the central university idea of Paris, Berlin and the like.

In all the politically important turning points, from the 1860s onward, the University, its teachers and students, have played a vital role at a national level and in expressing opinion. The establishing of new universities in various parts of Finland, especially from the 1960s onward, has affected the position of Helsinki University in teaching and research, but its status as the leading institution of academic culture, and as the standard bearer of social and international tradition, has been preserved. It is largely based on the importance of the student institutions.

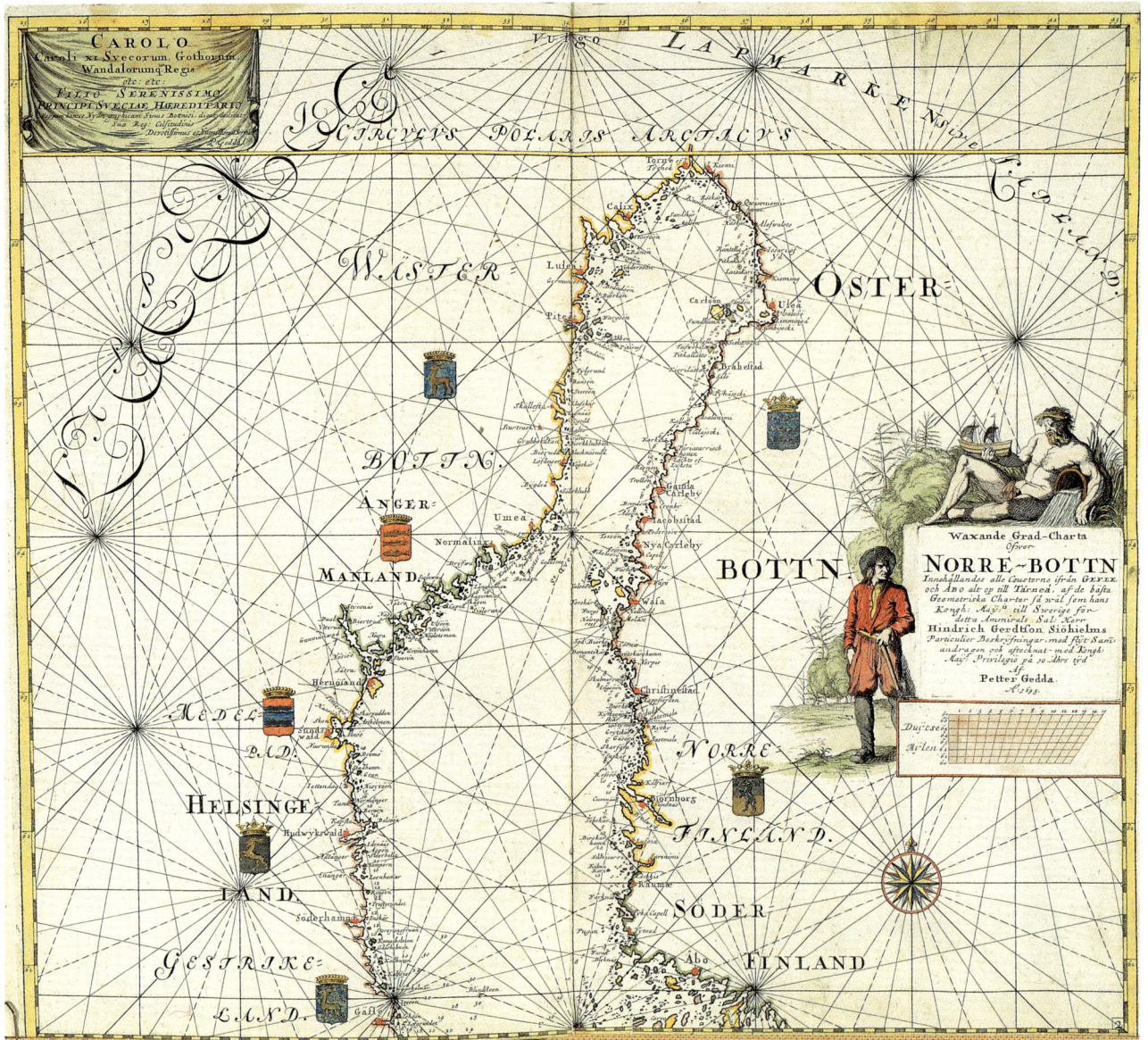

Old sea cards showing the Gulf of Bothnia are rare: the whole Gulf was closed to foreigners, and it did not have any greater military significance – it was an inland sea of the Swedish realm. There were several important cities on the coast of the Gulf of Bothnia, whose trade was controlled by Stockholm in the 17th century. It was not until the Diets of 1765–1766 that the chief towns on both sides of the Gulf were given the right to pursue foreign trade without the intervention of Stockholm. The chart was printed in Holland, 1694/95.

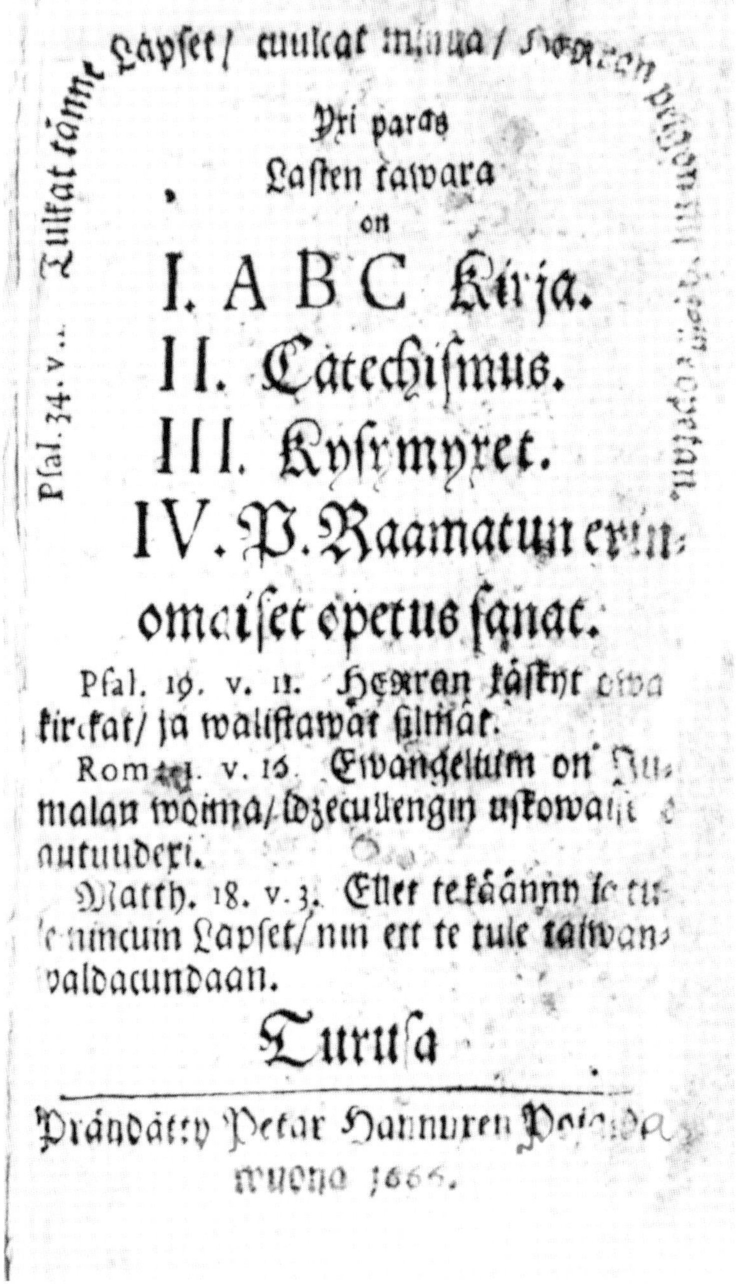

Tullkat tänne Lapset/ cuulcat minua/ Herran pelgon [illegible] opetan. Psal. 34. v. [illegible]

Yxi paras
Lasten tawara
on

I. A B C Kirja.
II. Catechismus.
III. Kysymyxet.
IV. P. Raamatun ercinomaiset opetus sanat.

Psal. 19. v. 11. Herran käskyt owat kirckat/ ja walistawat silmiät.

Rom. 1. v. 16. Ewangelium on Jumalan woima/ idzecullengin uskowaisel autuudexi.

Matth. 18. v. 3. Ellet te käänny ja tule nijncuin Lapset/ nijn ett te tule taiwan waldacundaan.

Turusa

Prändätty Petar Hannuxen Poialda
wuonna 1666.

Bishop Johannes Gezelius the Elder published a textbook of literacy and religion, The Children's Best Thing, *running to many editions. Its symbol is Psalm 34, verse 11, which in the Revised Standard Bible reads: Come O sons, listen to me, I will teach you the fear of the Lord.*

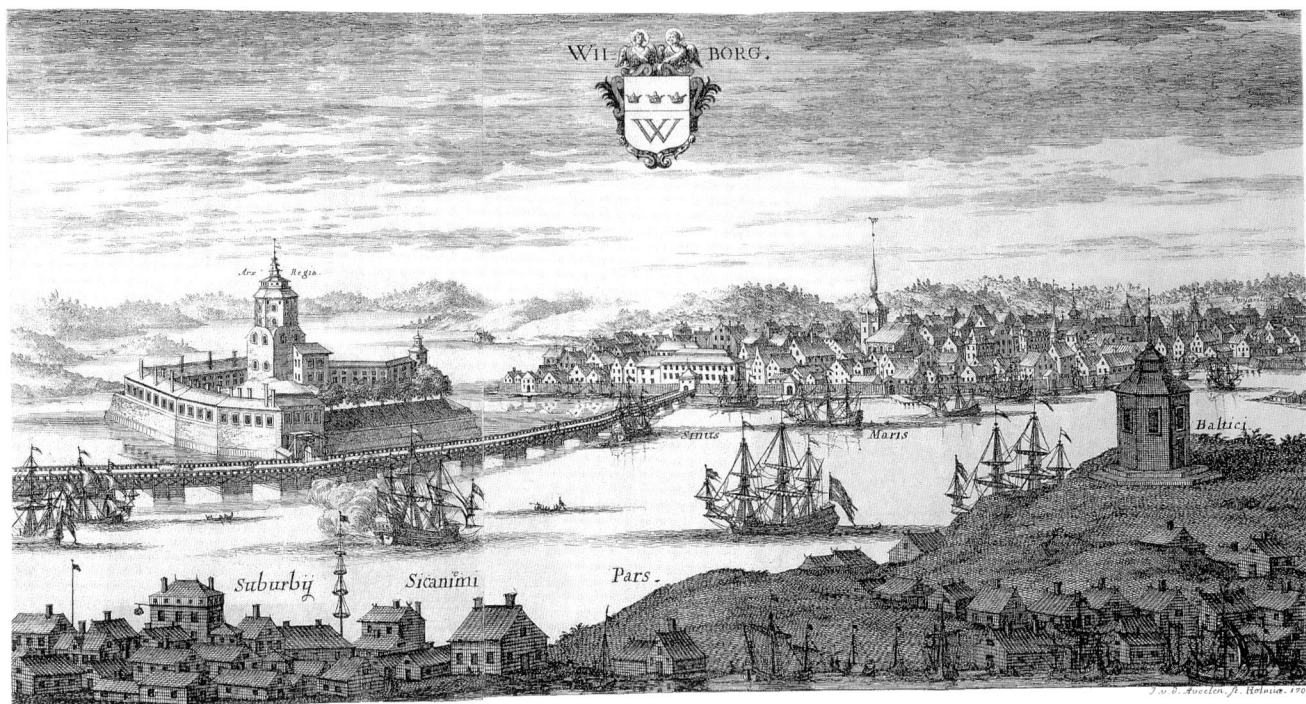

Owing to the Russian occupation, almost no pictures of Finnish territory appeared in the large illustrated work Suecia Antiqua et Hodierna *showing the Swedish kingdom in the beginning of the 18th century. There is one, however, of Viipuri, which in the picture of 1716 was in Russian hands, and remained there when peace was made in 1721. The picture shows the Viipuri coat-of-arms of three crowns, the old castle and the "Turku bridge", together with the city centre and its town hall; the suburb of Siikaniemi is in the foreground.*

period during which the country was, on several occasions, to enjoy the status of a special area of administration, Count Per Brahe, did much to advance the country's position. In being placed under the administration of a Governor-General, Finland was not, in fact, treated as a special case within the Kingdom, as other parts of the realm were also liable to be temporarily grouped into a district of special administration. During his first period of office, Brahe's area of administration comprised Finland and the province of Käkisalmi but not Ostrobothnia, while his second covered Finland and Ostrobothnia without the province of Käkisalmi. This is one indication of the fact that the name Finland had not yet taken on its present meaning.

There was a good deal of migration between the various parts of the Kingdom, and this had its effect on the relationship between the two languages. Since the Middle Ages Finns from the west had been moving into Sweden, and at the beginning of the 17th century large numbers of people migrated from Savo to western Sweden, where they gradually became absorbed into the Swedish-speaking population. Furthermore, centralization and the increased significance of Stockholm tended to strengthen the position of the Swedish language in Finland. Now and then, however, some attention was paid to the question of the ability of authorities in the Finnish-speaking area to use Finnish, and in the 18th century a translator was appointed to the Diet (the legislative assembly) for the benefit of the peasant representatives. In Stockholm, alongside the *Storkyrkan,* the Capital's most important church, there was also a Finnish church, which in fact still functions to this day. But it must be pointed out that, as the language of the Court and the nobility, German held an important position, as did Latin in University life.

RUSSIAN EXPANSION WESTWARDS IN THE 18TH CENTURY

Changes along the eastern border, tension and a relative decline in her importance within the Kingdom were features central to developments in Finland during the 18th century. As Russia grew in strength it began to expand to the west and in 1703 St. Petersburg was founded on territory that was still formally part of Sweden. In the Great Northern War which began in 1700, Russia occupied Estonia and Lithuania in addition to Ingria and Karelia and, from 1710 onwards, the whole of Finland as far as the Åland Islands and was even threatening the archipelago around Stockholm. The period of occupation, which was to be known as the Great Wrath, came to end with the Peace of Uusikaupunki (Nystad) in 1721 and with it came a redefinition of the Kingdom's eastern border and for Finland (without Karelia) once more under Swedish rule, a more peripheral position than before.

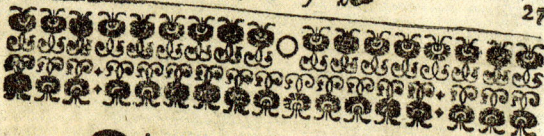

Die II Abtheilung.

Enthaltend eine Geographische Be-
schreibung der durch den Nystädtischen
Frieden respective cedirt-und restituirten
Provinzen.

Das Erste Capitel.

Von dem Groß-Herzogthum Finnland,
dessen theils Moscowitischen Provinzen, Ker-
holm und Carelien, theils Schwedischen, Nyland, Finnland, Cajanien, Savolaxien, Ta-
vasthlen; deren Lage, Gränzen, Eintheilung,
Fruchtbarkeit, vornehmsten Städten, Sit-
ten der Inwohnere und der-
gleichen.

Summarien.

1. Finnlandes Name 2. Grösse und Gränzen. 3. Frucht-
barkeit. 4. Hat sieben Provinzen. 5. Der I Provinz
Kexholm Gränzen und fata. 6. Fruchtbarkeit. 7.
Der See Ladoga. 8. Rubin-Bergwerke. 9. Die Städte/
Kexholm/ Taipol/ Systerbeck/ Petersburg/ Lexa.
10. Der II Provinz Carelien Gränzen / Namen und
fata. 11. Fruchtbarkeit. 12 Wiborg/ die Haupt-Stadt.
13. Von der wunderbaren Höhle bei Wiborg. 14. Die
Städte/ Mala/ und Wekelax. 15. Die III Provinz
Nyland. 16. Deren Städte/ Helsingfort/ Elimä/
Perno/

Following the major famine of the 1690's, a long war and a period of occupation, Finland's population and agriculture were in a poor state but, after the Treaty of Uusikaupunki, rural areas experienced a rapid revival, particularly the agricultural sector. The population of the area later to be known as Finland was about 390 000 in 1721, but by 1807 it had grown to 907 000. Development in the towns and in urban occupations was much slower. Despite a great number of new farms there was a rapid increase in the landless population and social divisions began to appear with a tenant farmer class emerging on the one hand and a group of wealthy peasants and *rusthollis* (holder of a farm under obligation to furnish and equip a cavalryman) on the other. Particularly towards the latter half of the 18th century there was a general improvement in the standard of living and this was naturally reflected in the sphere of culture.

During the war of reprisal known as the War of the Hats, between 1741 and 1743, Finland was once more occupied by Russia. Under the Treaty of Turku (1743), with the new border drawn along the River Kymi, Finland lost the Olavinlinna fortress along with the towns of Lappeenranta and Hamina, the latter of which had been built up as a port and fortress town to replace Wiborg, ceded to Russia under the Treaty of Uusikaupunki. At this time the idea was already being expressed that Finland should break away from Sweden. However, after the war, measures were taken to strengthen Finland's position within the realm, prominent among which were an economic development programme and the building of fortifications and naval fleet. The construction of Sveaborg (Viapori in Finnish, nowadays Suomenlinna) outside of Helsinki was a huge financial enterprise. Its very name indicates its wide national function. Economically and culturally Finland formed closer and closer links with Stockholm. Along with improvements in the standard of living and culture and better communications the Swedish language became more general. The effect of internal migration was felt particularly in the towns along the coast. A body of Finnish literature, mostly ecclesiastical and legal in nature, began to appear and for a short period a Finnish-language newspaper was published. The position of the Finnish language was recognized in the Diet and on bank notes, etc. but the increasing importance of the western parts of the Kingdom, including Gothenburg, pushed the whole of Finland and consequently the Finnish language into a more peripheral position. This was the main reason for the fact that the Finnish civil service became continuously more Finnish, that is to say that fewer and fewer officials came to Finland from other parts of the Kingdom.

The Regency, which reached the peak of its power towards the end of the 17th century, was superseded by the power of the Estates, the "Age of Freedom", which, in turn, came to an end with Gustavus III's coup d'état in 1772. The reign of Gustavus III and Gustavian culture were to be of importance to Fin-

After the loss of Viborg, Sweden built a new frontier fortress, named Fredrikshamn/ Hamina after the king. It was constructed completely according to the classical pattern: within the bastions a geometrical plan was formed. After the Peace of 1743, however, Hamina became a Russian frontier fortress, and after that from the 1820s it has been the cradle of training for Finnish regular and reserve officers. During the era of the Grand Duchy hundreds of Finnish officers of the Russian Imperial Army were trained at the Hamina Cadet School, and during the period of the Republic the Reserve Officer School has instructed thousands of officers.

A MAP or CHART of the GULFS of FINLAND AND LIVONIA with their respective Ports and Harbours Together with a large Plan of KROONSTAD AND S.t PETERSBURG Taken from an Original Drawing lately sent from S.t Petersburg.

GULF OF FINLAND

SWEDISH FINLAND

SOUTH FINLAND

NYLAND

RUSSIAN FINLAND

CARELIA

INGRIA

ESTHONIA

THE GULF OF LIVONIA

PART OF COURLAND

THE BALTICK SEA

THE NORTH BOTTOM

A Plan of KROONSTAD with the Port of S.t PETERSBURG.

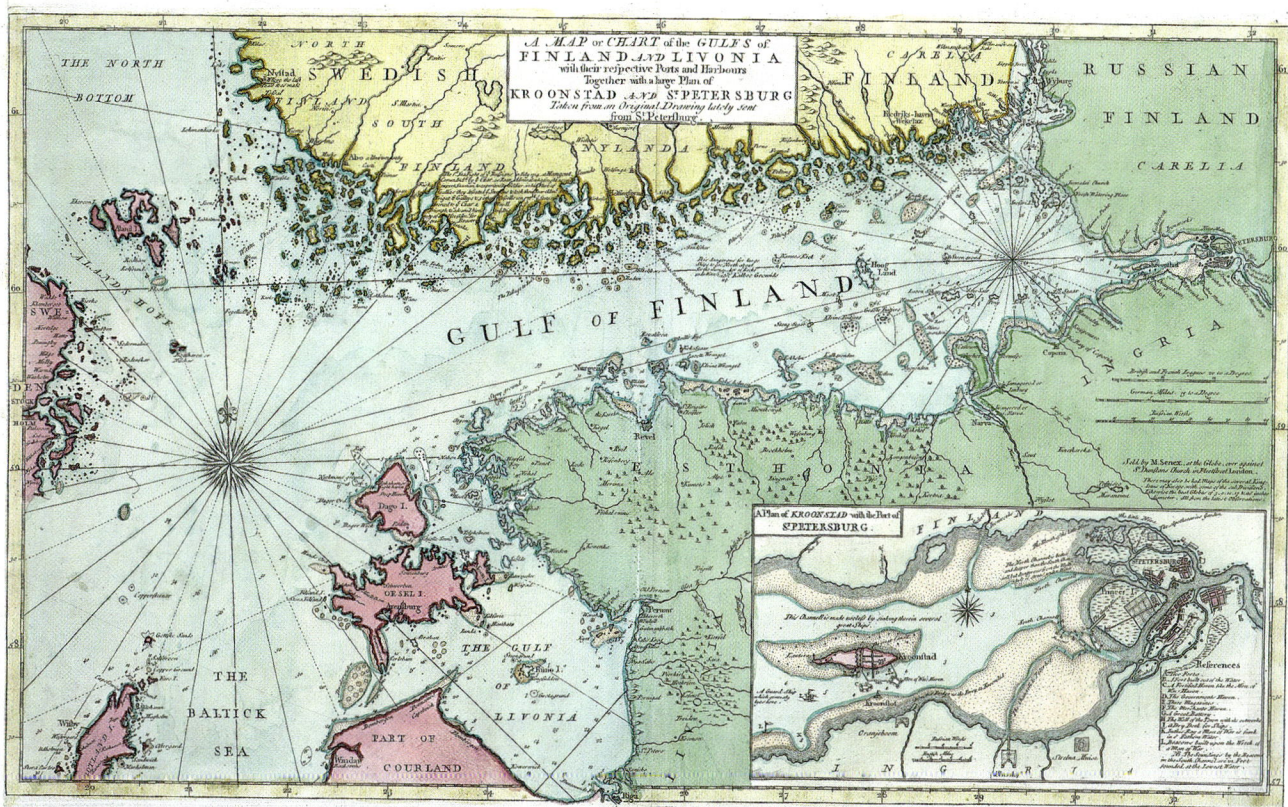

The sea area of the North Baltic and the Gulf of Finland had already been an important route for a thousand years when St. Petersburg's rise to become a great city in the 18th century increased its significance. With its archipelagos, shoals and low waters at its eastern end, the Gulf of Finland is, however, difficult to navigate, and many vessels – later interesting to marine archeologists – were wrecked in the autumn storms. The lighthouse system only developed slowly. The area in the picture was under dispute between Sweden and Russia throughout the 18th century; during the 19th century the "Pax Russica" prevailed here.

GUSTAF Den III.
Sveriges Gothes och Wendes Konung &c.
Arfvinge till Norrige, Hertig till Schleswig Holstein
Stormann och Dithmarsen Greve till Oldenburg och Delmenhorst.

Målad af L. Pasch   Graverat af Vollberg 1777

Gustavus III came to the
throne in 1771 and began
to implement the same
kind of tolerant and efficient programme in Swe-
den (-Finland) as his
uncle Frederick the Great
in Prussia. In the following year the king succeeded in vitally limiting parliamentary power. The
discontent of the aristo-
cratic opposition finally
led to the murder of the
king in 1792 at a Stock-
holm opera masked ball.
– Verdi composed an opera
on the subject.
The period of Gustavus
III saw a great break-
through of French culture
and Italian antiquity and
art; the kingdom became
stronger in financial and
military power.

Two big sea battles were fought at Ruotsinsalmi, (Svensksund) off the present city of Kotka, in the 1788–1790 war. The Russians won the first, the Swedes the second, under the leadership of King Gustavus III himself. Over 400 warships and 33 000 men took part in this great battle in July 1790. The picture shows big explosions and hits in the bombardment, together with large vessels of the open-sea fleet and, in the foreground, oar-propelled galley ships of the archipelago fleet.

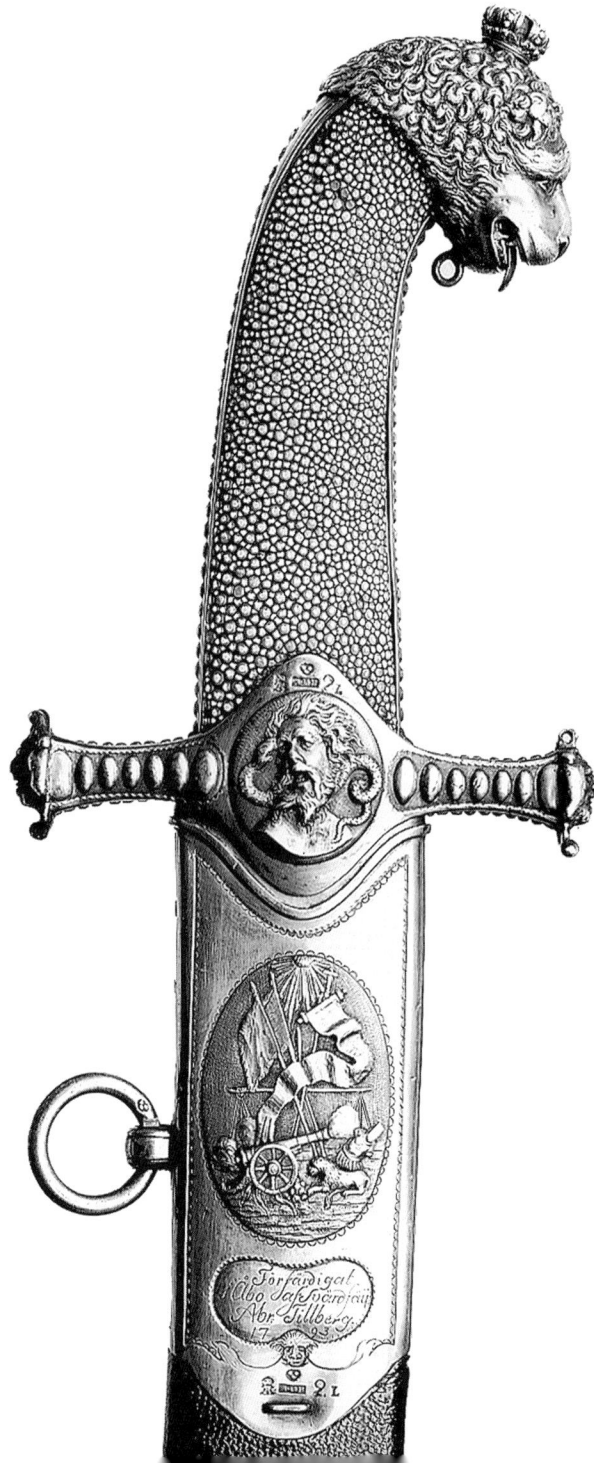

In 1793 the Turku master craftsman Abraham Tillberg made a fine sword for the young King Gustavus IV Adolphus, who was still a minor. The head of the sword hilt may be thought to refer to the Finnish Grand Duchy also, though the lion was the symbolic beast of the whole realm.

land and the reaffirmation of the power of the Regency was regarded as serving Finnish interests better than the power of the Diet. However, the nobility gradually rose up in opposition to the King as he began to limit the power of the Diet, simultaneously favouring those Estates of lower economic status. This development reached its peak in 1789 with the Act of Union and Security which was in the nature of a constitution and which the King sprang on the Diet as a kind of *fait accompli* in the middle of the war against Russia (1788–90).

During this war, which also developed into a war against Denmark, a separatist movement among army offices, with its roots in the opposition formed by the nobility, attempted to force the King to make peace by conducting separate negotiations with Russia. The origins of this officers' revolt (they were called the Anjala League) lay partly in plans, outlined a few years earlier by G. M. Sprengtporten, for an independent Finland under Russian suzerainty: these plans envisaged a nobility-centred form of government, based on ideas from the United States of America, resembling the Diet of the Age of Freedom. While they probably played a part in the way Finland's position would be organized between 1808 and 1809, these plans received little support during the war of 1788–1790.

But it is difficult to draw parallels between Finland's position as it was envisaged under Russian rule, with its government of nobles, and the reality of the country's subsequent history. Behind these events, which were tied up with the Anjala League, was the broad national constitutional opposition of the nobility to the power of the Regency. On the other hand, from Russia's point of view the plans to separate Finland from Sweden were of great significance. Following the subsequent Finnish war (1808–1809), fought against the background of the European power politics of the Napoleonic era, occupied Finland was no longer handed back to Sweden as it had been in 1721 and 1743, but was annexed by Russia as an autonomous "buffer state" with its own Diet and administration; Russia had, in fact, already considered the establishment of such a Diet during earlier periods of occupation in the 18th century. However, as the war indicates, there was a great deal of opposition to partition in Sweden and Finland. The reasons for Finland's separation from Sweden were not based on ethnical or linguistic principles or on the kind of nationalistic grounds that would appear later, neither was the border between Sweden and Russia (the Finnish Grand Duchy) drawn up on the basis of ethnic-linguistic considerations. It was not until after 1809 that a sense of Finnish identity began to develop, a trend which was later to embrace the kind of antiquarian interest that H. G. Porthan and his friends and pupils were to show in Finnish history, folklore and language during the latter part of the 18th century when the influence of the old University of Turku had been at its peak.

A painting by Isak Wacklin of Oulu, Miss Heckford's Portrait, *reveals the wide prevalence of rococo style. In the upper-class culture of the era women had an important role, from the Paris salons to the Russian Empresses.*

THE AUTONOMOUS GRAND DUCHY

In signing the Treaty of Tilsit in 1807, Czar Alexander I of Russia and Napoleon had come to an agreement on their respective spheres of interest, after which Russia had conquered Finland (1808–1809). Finland was of strategic importance to Russia because of its proximity to St. Petersburg. A hundred years earlier Peter the Great had conquered Karelia, Estonia and Lithuania and had founded his Capital on the territory he had taken. It was logical, therefore, to attempt to make the entire Gulf of Finland inaccessible to enemy fleets. Russia's front line of defence was brought up from Kronstadt to the Sveaborg (Suomenlinna) fortifications and even further to the west. In the 1830's work was begun on what was planned to be the major fortification of Bomarsund on the Åland Islands. With its sparse population and its poverty, Finland as such did not interest Russia, but after the establishment of St. Petersburg Russia needed to protect its western capital and ensure access

Baron Gérard was called "the painter of kings and the king of painters"; the portrait of Alexander I is one of his best works. The young Emperor is shown against a background of the stormy weather of the times, a gentle conqueror, majestic but human. The picture belongs to Helsinki University, one of the most valuable works of the Alexander University.

During the period when Sweden was a really great power in the 17th century, the Baltic was almost an inland sea of the Swedish kingdom; only the southern coastline, from Courland to Prussia, from parts of Poland and Germany to Denmark belonged to others. Even there Sweden had conquered Pomerania and Skåne.

The map shows the location of Sveaborg (Suomenlinna) off Helsinki: islands sheltered the vessels anchored on the inside, but it is also possible to reach directly to the open sea via the sounds between the islands. Thus the fortress served the benefit of both the open-sea sailing fleet as well as the oar-propelled archipelago fleet, and enabled effective attacks eastward. It was intended to build fortifications on the mainland side also, to prevent a possible landing and attack from the land. The enemy did press from there in 1808, however, and the fortress had to surrender. Extensive encircling fortifications were not built until World War I.

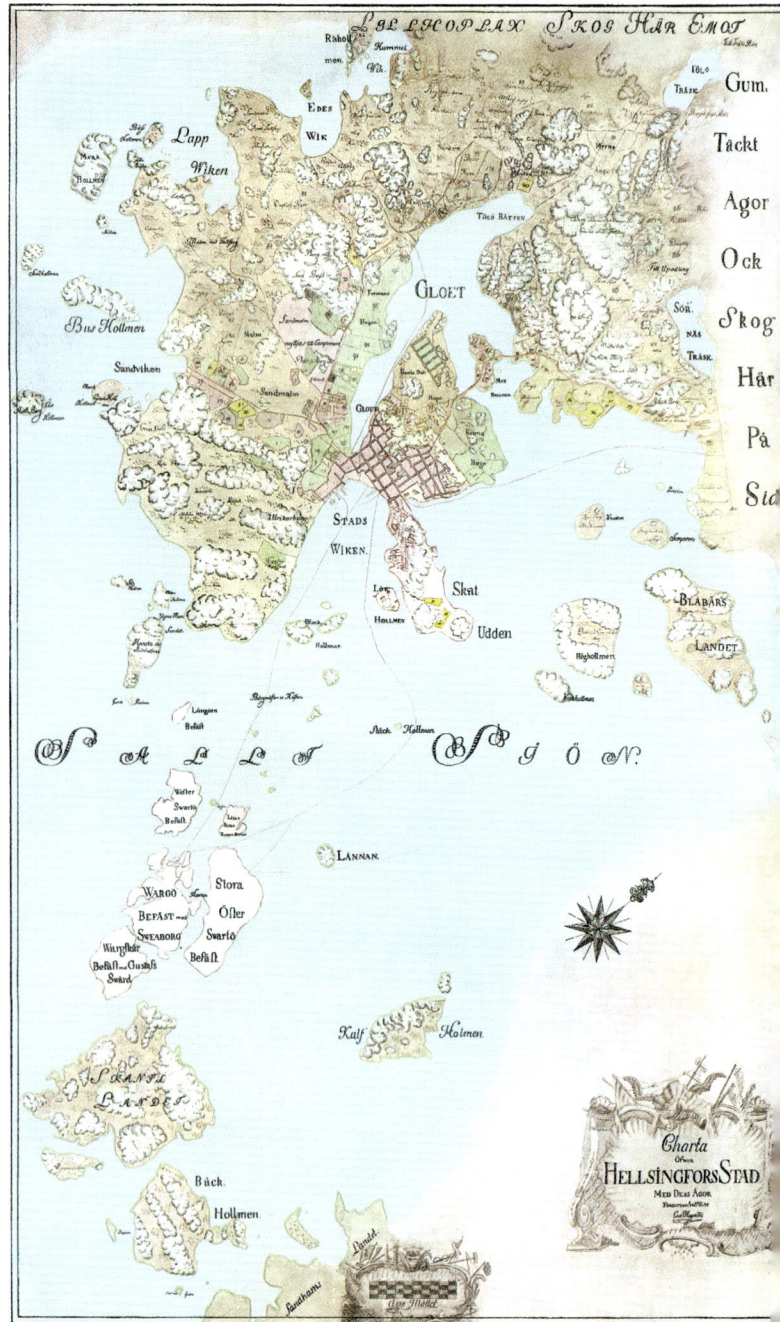

From 1617 Russia had no contact at all with the Baltic coast.

Czar Peter I began a new period in Russian foreign and military policy by expanding his country to the shores of both the Baltic and the Black Sea, and by establishing naval fleets on both seas.

The Baltic policy of Peter I also from the first was marked by a strong trade and cultural bias. The fortification of St. Petersburg (Sankt Peterburg) and the Kronstadt sea fortress outside it, founded in 1703, were to protect the swiftly growing great city which in 1712 replaced Moscow as the capital and administrative centre of all Russia.

The importance of the Finnish Gulf area changed vitally when Russia thus succeeded in reversing the centuries-old expansion of Sweden from west to east.

The Peace of Nystad in 1721 confirmed the rule of Czar Peter the Great over Estonia, Livonia, Ingria (where the city of St. Petersburg was established), Karelia (including Viipuri) and the whole of Lake Ladoga – and won him the title of *imperator*. The Nystad border became the new key to the strategic security identity of Russia; in particular it set Stalin's aim in the wars between Finland and the Soviet Union 1939-1945, and achieved it was as far as Finland was concerned – as with Estonia and Livonia. (Russia lost the latter in 1991).

Thus the same situation prevailed in the Finnish Gulf area: its northern and southern shores belonged to different realms; between them there was a strained relationship leading both to efforts to establish peace and to wars, with both sides building fortifications and equipping fleets. This had a vital effect on the development of Helsinki.

Russia's chief opponent in European power politics was Turkey, supported by France. Sweden abandoned its policy of conciliation towards Russia in the 1730s, and due to French pressure joined the French-Turkish front. Because of this Sweden launched a retaliatory war on Russia in 1741, with the purpose of winning back the areas lost in the Great Northern War. But the Russians won the war, and the border was moved westward, to Kymijoki. The policy of the French alliance adopted was, however, continued, and Sweden prepared for new wars in the Gulf of Finland. The aim when war broke out was to compel Russia to fight on two fronts, against both Sweden and Turkey; this indeed proved to be what happened.

This makes it understandable why France had good reason to pay Sweden considerable subsidies. From 1748 these were chiefly used to build the great fortress of *Sveaborg-Viapori-Suomenlinna*, on the islands of *Vargskär* off Helsinki, and a fleet for it. The pur-

pose of the project was to prevent new Russian efforts to occupy Finland, but above all it was intended as a base for offensive operations against St. Petersburg.

Sveaborg, given the name of Suomenlinna in 1918 and today part of the UNESCO World Heritage programme, is an interesting memorial of military architecture and great garrisons. But visitors today do not see the hundreds of open-sea sailing ships of varying sizes that were a vital part of it, and especially the typical light galleys designed for the Finnish archipelago, and remain unaware of their sounds, smells and seamen.

Although Russia invested on a considerable scale to strengthen the Kronstadt fortress, the Tallin and other fortifications opposite Helsinki, and its fleet, Sveaborg was a permanent threat from the initial years of the late 18th century. In 1788 Sweden (again together with Turkey) attacked Russia, once more with the intention of winning both the lands it had lost and trying together with Turkey to weaken and divide Russia otherwise. War at sea was particularly in question, the main battles being near Suursaari (Hogland) and Kotka. But Sweden did not succeed in its aims this time either.

In 1806–1807 Napoleon's army conquered Prussia and reached the Baltic coast. Russia had to change its policy, and in

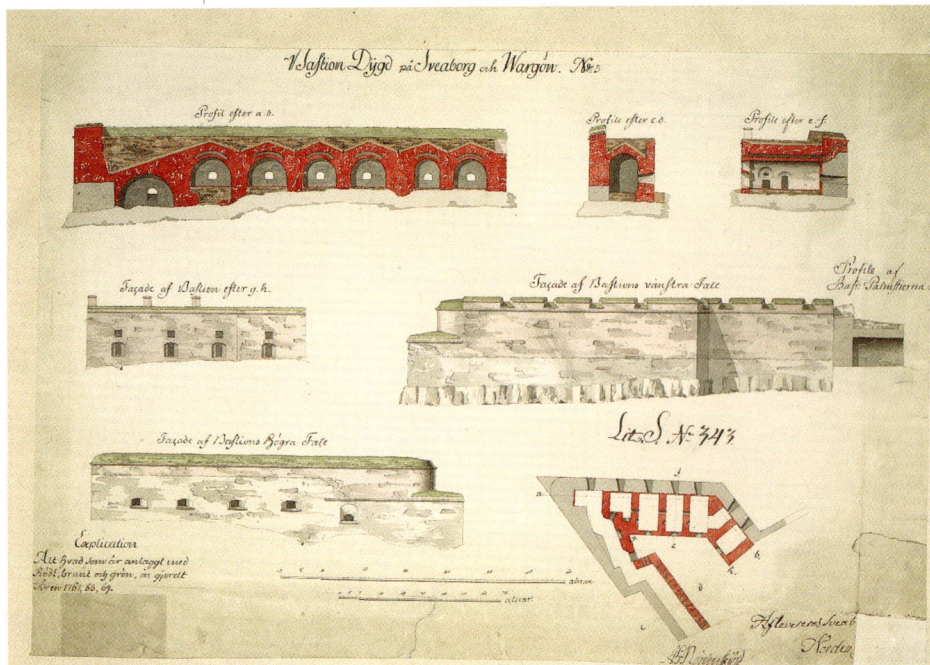

Profil efter a.b.

Profile efter c.d.

Profile efter e.f.

Façade af Bastion efter g.h.

Façade af Bastions vänstra Fate

Profile af Baß. Palustierna.

Façade af Bastions Högra Fate

Litz S. N° 343.

Explication
Alt hvad som är anlagt med Rödt, brant och grön, är gjordt Åren 1767, 68, 69.

Suomenlinna (Sveaborg) was built according to French fortifications architecture on rocky outer islands; the bastions are comparatively low. The fortress was equipped with over a thousand guns, and in addition vessels were armed. Posterity must imagine the great fort with all its garrison and sailing ships, with its clamour and smells. The atmosphere of Suomenlinna when it was in action differed entirely from the peaceful idyll tourists now encounter. The garrison trained, weapons were transported, ships were tarred, sails were sewn.

1807 Czar Alexander I and Emperor Napoleon I concluded the Alliance of Tilsit, on the border of Lithuania and Prussia. It was agreed there that Russia should join in a mercantile war against Britain and the effort to divide the Turkish realm. Russia had a free hand in overthrowing England's ally, Sweden; in 1808 Alexander I essentially beat "his geographical enemy" and announced that he was annexing Finland to Russia permanently. The key point was the Sveaborg fortress: it was this threat that Russia wanted to eliminate, and when it had been isolat-

ed and it surrendered after a siege in May 1808, there was a big victory parade in St. Petersburg, and Russia desired that salutes should be fired in Paris also in honour of the occasion.

Thanks to the building of Sveaborg and the importance of the large garrison, Helsinki grew to be a significant though not a large city in the latter part of the 18th century. The cultural style of Sveaborg was essentially a continuation of Stockholm culture, of the nobility and high society, with its freemason lodges, masked balls, novels and music. The atmos-

phere of Sveaborg differed from that of Turku and Porvoo – cities of bishops and study. Many officers had served in the Strasbourg *Royal Suédois* regiment, and Sveaborg talked military and power politics. Unlike the clergy and farmers of the countryside, who were royalists, the officers favoured the aristocratic opposition expressed during the Russian war of Gustavus III in the Anjala league's opposition of 1789 and finally in the murder of the king in 1792.

The self-portrait of the Finnish painter B. Goden-hjelm was painted when he was studying at the St. Petersburg Imperial Academy of Arts. The interior is in the Empire or Biedermeier spirit with its antique-style pillars. The portrait of the Emperor is in the background on a pedestal, but a partially visible portrait of a Polish nobleman represents the interest of the times in history and the loving couple in the foreground the romantic mainstream.

to the Baltic Sea. Sweden, its period as a great power at an end, no longer constituted any great danger, but what Russia did consider a danger was the possibility that during a major war Sweden, or later an independent Finland, by forming alliances with Russia's enemies, would provide them with a base from which to attack. It was Sweden's alliance with Great Britain, the enemy of France and Russia (now enjoying friendly relations), that was behind the war of 1808–1809.

A very important aspect of Russia's annexation of Finland was the way in which it was carried out and the form that Finnish society assumed as a result. As such, it was not exceptional that Finland was allowed to retain its own legislation and its own form of society since many other countries annexed by Russia earlier, including the Baltic states, had kept their own forms of government, and in 1815 Poland too retained its status as a separate kingdom within the Russian Empire. Finland's position was confirmed, with the war still in progress, at the grand Duchy's first separate Diet held in Porvoo, at which time the Czar proclaimed Finland's "elevation to national status". Russia was not a united centralized state, neither was it united nationally or religiously. Thus, from the Russian point of view there was nothing peculiar or exceptional in Finland's Lutheran Church. However, in relation to Russia, Finland's position regarding its internal affairs was one of considerable independence, evidently for the reason that, in certain respects,

In 1809 a Government Council was established for Finnish internal administration, soon to be given the name of the Imperial Finnish Senate. A special uniform was ratified for its members, the Senators.

The French Revolution affected the whole world, and as early as the 1790s the "Marseillaise" was translated even into Finnish. The revolutionary poem was strictly forbidden in Sweden, and Henrik Achrenius hardly expected it to be published. But it is an important sign of the spreading of ideals. Achrenius was police superintendent at Kalajoki, Ostrobothnia.

it served as a model area from the point of view of the liberal policies that Alexander I was pursuing at the time. The free status of the Finnish peasantry and their representation in the Diet was of particular importance to Alexander and his plans to carry out reforms throughout the Realm, plans which were interrupted by Napoleon's attack in 1812. Finland not only retained its Lutheran religion, Swedish as its official language, its old Swedish system of civil and criminal law, but also its Gustavian form of government, the adaptation of which to Finnish circumstances together with the fact that Finland had its own central administration headed by the Senate and, in principle, its own Diet with its four Estates, meant the birth of a separate Finnish state. Finland had, of old, held the heraldic status of a Grand Duchy, now it became a Grand Duchy de facto, with its own insitution. The autocratic Czar of Russia agreed, by way of an "experiment" to become the constitutional monarch of Finland and Poland. From here it was intended that this system be extended to cover the whole of Russia. However, due to changing circumstances in Europe this did not materialize and, as a result of the uprisings in 1830 and 1863, Poland lost its Parliament and its special status. The Finns, who remained loyal and rather conservative throughout the 19th century, had what were on the whole rather favourable conditions to develop a state which had come into being as the result of Great power politics and which, although it did not constitute an

Finnish industry started with ironworks. On the Finnish side there was some ore, but especially forests and water power; the bulk of the ore was brought from the Swedish archipelago by water. The Fagervik ironworks community with its manor and church on the Uusimaa coast.

The seal of the Societas Scientiarum Fennica, Finland's oldest academy of science, founded in 1838.

ethnic totality, was nevertheless a geographically viable entity. Dialects of Finnish were spoken on both the Swedish and Russian sides of the border and, in Finland itself, in addition to the Swedish-speaking or bilingual upper classes, there was considerable Swedish-speaking rural population. Alexander had wanted the state to include the Swedish-speaking Åland Islands but not the Finnish-speaking area of Länsipohja (Westrobothnia); what was involved was the forming of a strategic and not expressly an ethnic entity. As far as trade and communications were concerned, western Finland inclined towards Sweden, eastern Finland more and more towards St. Petersburg. Later, the network of roads and canals, and particularly the coming of the railroad, would support the tendency of administration to centralize in a way counter to the disintegrative hull of these major commercial centres.

A clear indication of Russia's desire to make an independently functioning entity of Finland was the creation of the area's own capital. Under Swedish rule, Turku, with its Bishop's Seat, its University and its Court of Appeals, had been the centre of the province, but Finland's capital had, of course, been Stockholm. Now, with the decision to make Helsinki the new administrative centre, (1812), a new capital was created. Helsinki had been burnt down during the war and now it was re-built in an unprecedentedly handsome fashion to show both Finns and the outside world that a new political unit, the Grand

In the 18th century the whole of Finland came under the Stockholm sphere of influence, not only administratively and politically but also economically and culturally. Stockholm was thus the Finnish capital in every respect; even in the academic world the Stockholm Royal Academy of Science and the Royal Academy of Literature (*Vitterhetsakademien*) were important centres.

The new Grand Duchy of Finland maintained significant ties with Sweden, whose own and translated literature and press were vitally important in Finland. But the building and cultural rise of a new capital, Helsinki, in the 1830s and 1840s no longer reflected Swedish influences. Instead, German models became important.

The architect C.L. Engel, born

The Orthodox Church of the capital is on the left-hand side of the picture, and opposite it the hospital of the Russian garrison with its sentry boxes, today the History department of the University Topelia complex. The allegorical reliefs of the facade have been destroyed. To the right seems to be walking one of the Russian traders who has come to the city.

In 1844 the library building of the Imperial Alexander University was completed; it is one of Engel's finest creations and an outstanding example of Helsinki architecture. Venny Soldan-Brofeldt's water-colour shows a copy of the Laocoon statue in the background, brought to Finland in the 1840s and paid for with money collected by students.

in Berlin, was offered a unique opportunity to design and build the new capital, and then as head of building operations to plan and direct other town planning and building in the whole country. When big fires destroyed several cities, Engel's hand could be seen especially in the planning of Turku

and Oulu; also in the designing of numerous churches and manors.

Engel's letters to Berlin give us the opportunity of following its activities and enthusiasm, and at the same time the concrete and well-informed interest that the Emperors Alexander I and Nicholas I showed in his work. Especially Nicholas I was artistically talented and had been given architectural training as a fortifications officer. The monumental centre of Helsinki created by Engel is indeed a permanent memorial of the era of Alexander and Nicholas.

Engel's architectural message was purely classical. The style cultivating the Middle Ages and "Tudor" romance that had become prevalent in Western Europe did not arouse much interest in Finland, before the neo-Renaissance style became the dominant form of expression in Finnish cities. Classicism was in keeping with the policy of the Russian government and governments of other countries of the Holy Alliance, whose main object was to prevent a new outbreak of the French Revolution and similar rebellious movements in Europe. The aim was economic and social reforms without revolutionary ideology, with a high-level body of civil servants. It was therefore advisable to stress the status of the University in all respects.

An essential part of civil servant education was the study of political philosophy, from the beginning of the 1830s through the Hegelian system in particular. The leading professors of philosophy and history were Hegelians; this meant the setting aside of German and Swedish idealistic philosophy. Scarcely anywhere else did Hegelian philosophy gain such a dominant position as in Finland, where it found a significant developer and adapter in J.V. Snellman. Snellman was already Finland's most important journalist in the 1840s, and as soon as Alexander II came into power he was invited in 1856 to be a professor of philosophy, and then in 1863 a member of the Imperial Senate of the Finnish government. Later he continued as an active writer. In the spirit of Hegel, Snellman developed systematic political thinking, endeavouring to see the most important lines in both social and political relations, and opposing the idealism linked with romantic ideals.

In the world of music the influences of the German and the older and new romantic school rapidly came to the fore. Friedrich (Fredrik) Pacius, born in Hamburg, achieved the same kind of monopoly in Finnish music as Engel in architecture. As a university music teacher he trained a choir capable of performing great oratorios, developed an orchestra, composed and rehearsed the first – surprisingly high-level – Finnish operas and musical plays, and in the revolutionary year of 1848 introduced the Finnish national anthem *Our Land* to Runeberg's words. Pacius made the University Festival Hall the most important Finnish concert hall for over a century, and began to educate Finnish music audiences and critics.

Luther is the early great name of German influence in Finland; after religion followed the philosophy of Hegel, and in the next phase was the considerable technical influence of Germany, best represented by the Siemens enterprise. At the end of the 19th and the beginning of the 20th centuries, there were significant German influences in all fields of science and new ideals, the most important being various forms of socialism.

The year 1863 is memorable in Finnish political history. Under the patronage of Alexander II, Finnish parliamentary life was reborn then. In the 1860s Finland obtained many reforms demanded by the times, its own currency, the official legalization of the Finnish language, and limited company, municipal and Church legislation. It was vital that Finland remained loyal to Russia, contrary to the rebellious Poland. A polonaise version of the Our Land *anthem that became a vital symbol reveals the enthusiasm of the memorable year.*

Duchy of Finland, had come into being. It was then that those institutions and, to a great extent, the buildings which still today house Finland's central administration were created. The President's office is of course in the former palace of the Czar.

The building up and the preservation of Finland's institutions and her special status was the oldest bureaucratic means of forming a national identity. With the exception of a Governor-General, the representative of the Czar, the Finnish civil service was com-

Imatrankoski waterfall bursts through the Salpausselkä geological formation in Southeast Finland, to the north of which lies the broad lakeland of Finland. Imatra became a famous sight of the romantic 19th century, attracting people from St. Petersburg especially. Through Imatra the waters of the Finnish interior run into Lake Ladoga and from there via the Neva to the sea at St. Petersburg. Completed in 1856, the Saimaa Canal was excavated somewhat to the west of Imatra; this connects a lake route of over 400 km to the sea at Viipuri.

Elias Lönnrot på vandring.
Teckning af A. V. Linsén.

The most important collector of ancient Finnish poetry was the doctor and later professor of Finnish Elias Lönnrot. From disconnected poems he created, largely following Homeric models, a Finnish national epic, the Kalevala *(1835, 1848). The early 19th century was a time of great and partly unauthentic national epics everywhere.*

posed entirely of native Finns. But it was only with the convening of the Diet that wider circles could make themselves felt. The Diet, which had assembled only once before, in Porvoo in 1809, was convened again in 1863 during Alexander II's period of liberalization, and from then on at regular intervals. With Europe experiencing a period of political reaction, Finland came under the severe and patriarchal rule of Czar Nicholas I. But Nicholas respected Finland's special status and during his reign a number of writers whose work went a long way to creating a sense of national unity in Finland emerged alongside the bureaucracy. J. L. Runeberg, Finland's national poet, in such works as *The Elk skiers* and *Tales of Ensign Stål* created an idealized picture of a poor but industrious Finish people living in harmony and contentment. These works contain an elevated but humane and often humorous description of the people, and includes what was to become the Finnish national anthem, "Maamme" (Our Land), in which the beauty of Finland's summer landscape becomes the object of love of the fatherland. Alongside the works of Runeberg, the body of Finnish folklore collected and presented in poetic form by Elias Lönnrot was to be of the greatest significance. This collection, the Finnish national Epic, the *Kalevala,* did much to spread an awareness of Finland's existence and special character throughout Europe in spite of the fact that, from the point of view of the emergent Finnish culture and even the Finnish language, the folklore on

The Finnish identity was not built on history, but on landscape and poetry. When the Grand Duchy of Finland was formed in 1809, the image of Finnishness was no longer per se acceptable or sufficient as reflected during its six hundred years as a part of the Swedish realm. Belonging to the Russian Empire was something new; it did not mean an ethnic and historical linking with Russianness – such a national feeling was only beginning to develop in Russia itself. Emperor Alexander I and his closest advisers already desired to develop a separate Finnish identity. It was to be both monarchic and popular, to favour the Finnish language and Finnish folk traditions, and to be separated from Swedishness. The revolution in Stockholm and the election of a new ruling family (Bernadotte) also liberated Finns from feelings of loyalty to the new, small state of Sweden, and culturally it was considered advisable to turn primarily to German influences.

Although Finnish had already become a written language in the 1540s, it had not been developed into a modern cultural language, and at the beginning of the 19th century there were few educated people who could write Finnish. Attempts to publish Finnish-language newspapers were, however, made from the late 1810s onward; at the same time the first small selections of Finnish folk poetry appeared.

Interest in folk poetry was a great ideal everywhere in Europe in the 1820s. Special interest was aroused by Serbian folk poetry and the Greek War of Independence, which from the Western European standpoint was linked to the literary tradition of ancient Greece. Among the first poetic works of the future national poet, J.L. Runeberg,

The Finnish national poet J.L. Runeberg created an ideal picture of the Finnish nation and the Finnish landscape – an uninhabited panorama landscape of summer Finland arousing moral and religious feelings. Runeberg's programme was consciously anti-revolutionary; he wrote his great landscape poems during the period of unrest, 1846–1853. Edelfelt's illustration of Runeberg's Tales of Ensign Stål.

was in fact a selection in Swedish of Serbian folk poetry, in 1830. In his epic poem *The Elk Skiers*, written in hexameters, Runeberg drew an idyllic, harmonious picture of Finnish folk life, which completely differed from earlier characterizations emphasizing sloth and primitiveness. At the same time Runeberg's friend E. Lönnrot collected all the known Finnish folk runes, discovered a large amount of epic folklore beyond the Finnish eastern border, in Russian Karelia, and composed from these materials a coherent epic, *Kalevala*, whose first version appeared in 1835–1836, (a final, greatly expanded version was published in 1849). Lönnrot then published an extensive collection of lyrical poems, *Kanteletar* (1840), while Runeberg developed his interpretation of the Finnish character oriented towards "the noble poor" and an artistic atmosphere in the Greek spirit.

Alongside the idealizing of the folk character and folk poetry, there developed an interpretation of Finland as a moral landscape, and a panorama opening out from high over lakes and ridges became an essential element of Finnishness. Runeberg was already writing of it in the 1830s, and it became a central theme of his poem *Our Land*, written in 1846 and to become a national song with its 11 stanzas in the revolution of 1848. Its message is the welding of patriotism with Finland's harsh but beautiful landscape, its hills, wooded heaths, islands and lakes – scenic elements expressing the harmony and nobleness of simplicity, in contrast to the wastefulness and luxury of other countries. This moral interpretation of landscape fitted in well with the Finnish conservative policy of loyalism, and largely directed Finnish student youth to national Finnishness instead of European revolutionism.

Later this landscape world became important in the nationally significant Finnish painting, and later a significant element of photography and tourist advertising, as also of the way Finns spend their summers. Finland was presented not only to Finns but even more to foreigners as the land of forest and lakes: pictures do not show people or houses, still less factories or cities.

Eero Järnefelt's autumn landscape, painted in 1899, of Koli in North Karelia, belongs to the era of enthusiasm about Karelia – Karelianism. Järnefelt wanted to show the same grandeur in the landscape as the Kalevala was thought to represent. Karelianism associated the Kalevala particularly with Karelia and East Karelia, archaic backwoods. A parallel phenomenon can be observed in the Kalevala music composed at the same time by Järnefelt's brother-in-law, Jean Sibelius.

which it is based played a peripheral and receding role. It was not so much the contents or the language of the *Kalevala* which gave its publication such importance but the fact that Finns had been capable of such a cultural achievement. As distinct from Sweden, Finland had no history of its own, and (in a Romantic age, in which history, the Gothic and old ruins played an important role in the emergence of a national identity in many other countries) very few historical monuments. Thus Runeberg's "antique" concept of man and his idealization of the Finnish landscape together with the existence of the *Kalevala* were long to form the basis of a sense of Finnish national identity. It was only at the turn of the century that the *Kalevala,* as a source of inspiration to the masters of the "Golden Age" of Finnish art, was to have an important impact on Finnish culture.

The fact that the country had only one University to train the entire future civil service was an important factor in bringing about Finnish unity. The University held a central position in the country's intellectual life since outside its circles cultural resources were few. There were no large cities and no wealthy bourgeoisie, the nobility was small in number and the clergy was dispersed throughout the country. However, the University, which received the strong support of the government, did provide the prerequisites for literary and scientific study and the organizations connected to the University were the only forums in which political debate was possible. Thus the

Students drinking toasts in a Helsinki restaurant in the 1840s.

University fulfilled an important function in training and supplying the human capital for the debate periods of the 1840's and for the critical years of the 1860's. A considerable proportion of the staff of the new Diet, of the journalists of the political and literary press and even of those people involved in creating a new era in art and industry were products of the University.

Along with the University, another important educational channel during Finland's period of autonomy was the Imperial Army. At the beginning of the 19th century one in five sons of the nobility, later

Many Finns benefited from the Russian empire. The sons of Finland's few aristocrats and others often served in the Russian army, and – thanks to their Lutheran standards of work and abilities – rose to high rank. One of the last of them was Baron Gustaf Mannerheim, who became a Lieutenant-General in the Russian army. In the picture he is a colonel, commander of the 13th Uhlan regiment stationed in Poland, 1909. He later became Commander-in-Chief in the Finnish War of Independence – Civil War of 1918, in the Winter War 1939–1940 and the Continuation War 1941–1944, the Lapland War 1944–1945, Regent of Finland 1919 and President 1944–1946. He was made Field-Marshal in 1933 and Marshal of Finland in 1942.

one in nine, served in the Russian army, as did many outside the nobility, and Finland had its own Cadet School. The fact that about four hundred out of a total of some 3000 Finnish soldiers are known to have reached the rank of General or Admiral is a measure of their success. Many of these soldiers returned to Finland to take up posts in the civil service or to work in industry or other professions. Their period of service and the high-level training they received in different positions in the army of what was perhaps the most powerful state in the world brought the kind of insight and experience to Finland that did much to prevent the intellectual isolation which otherwise threatens a small country. The best-known figure to have chosen this path was the Finnish Field-Marshal, Mannerheim.

In spite of its autonomy Finland was not separated from Russia in other respects. Men from the local Russian garrisons were common sights in many Finnish towns. Along with them came Russian merchants and through their influence Orthodox churches were built. On the other hand there was a constant flow of people from eastern Finland to St. Petersburg, where they either settled permanently or returned a few years later. The St. Petersburg economy, in other ways too, had a great influence on Finland.

The reign of Alexander II (1855–81), and in particular the 1860's, was a period of considerable liberalization in Finland, where reforms went on even after Russia itself had turned in a more conservative direction. The most important reform concerned the Diet. Following the convening of a preparatory committee in January 1861, the Diet of 1863–64 was held in Helsinki as were all subsequent ones. The rules of procedure for the Diet, which contained Four Estates until 1906, were enacted in 1869. Thus, at the beginning of the century, the bureaucratic society was being replaced by a civic society, one in which, it is true, the right to vote in matters of state was extended to only a very small section of the people, depending on the composition of the various Estates. The change-over to a new form of society was advanced by decrees granting self-administration to the provinces, universal freedom to ply a trade, permission to establish banks and limited companies, equal rights of inheritance to women, and by the removal of education from the control of the Church, as well as a great many other reforms. From the 1860's onwards the establishment of numerous companies, societies and newspapers heralded the arrival of a new era.

The fact that new forms of livelihood were encouraged can be seen not only in the legislation of the time but also in policies regarding transport and communications. At the beginning of the 19th century, with the purchasing of coastal steamers and the building of canals, great strides were made in developing water traffic. The Saimaa Canal, an important Finnish waterway, was opened in 1856. Towards the

OM FINLANDS FLAGGA

af oſs föreslagen   af Dagbladet.

HELSINGFORS.
Finska Litt. Sällsk. Tryckeri-Bolag.

Liberal enthusiasm in the 1860s included exaggerated ideas about Finland's constitutional status, possible neutrality and its own flag. A big debate over the flag question arose, and numerous proposals were made, but the matter was soon buried. Blue and white began to be the Finnish national colours, but the Liberals preferred the coat-of-arms' combination of red and yellow as more historical and non-Russian. The dispute culminated in the phase of Finland's independence, 1917–1918, when the flag colours were first red and yellow, but immediately afterwards blue and white.

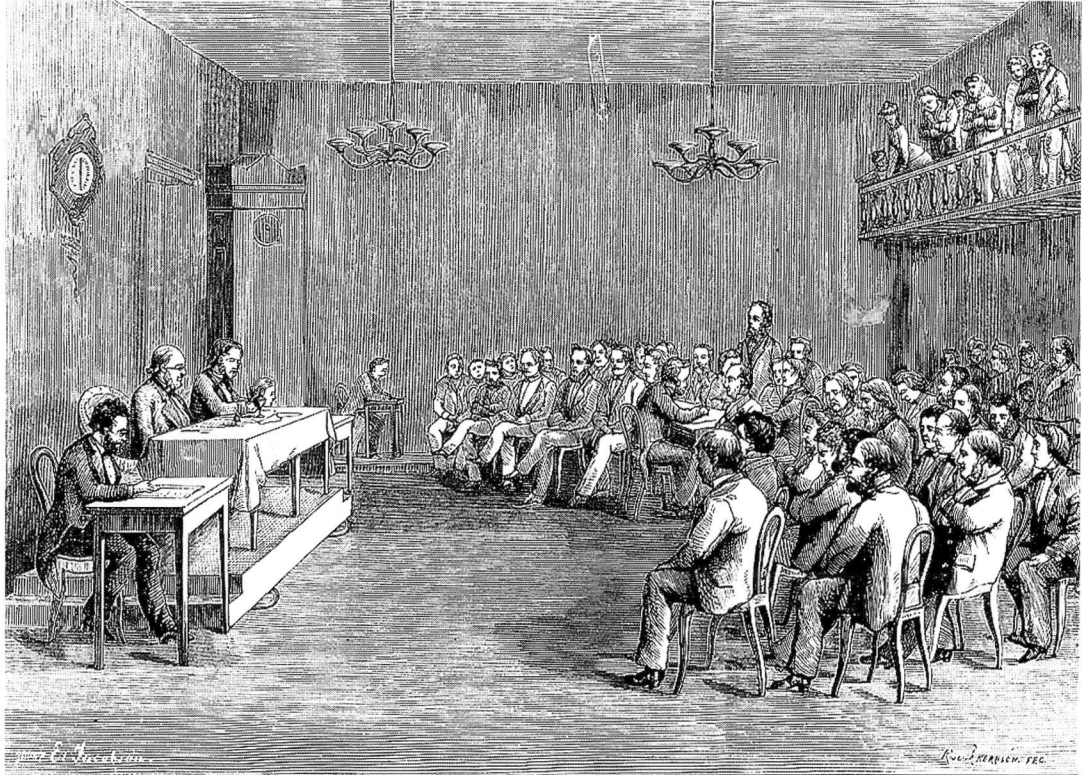

The Emperor could not allow Russia (or Poland) a parliament until 1906, but he could revive the old Diet of the Four Estates in Finland, which met regularly from 1863; thus the Emperor-Grand Duke was Finland's constitutional ruler. In the picture a session of the Farmers' Estate; sessions of the Aristocracy, the Clergy and the Bourgeoisie were pictured in more impressive surroundings. Handsome buildings were later built for the Estates in Helsinki, but the single-chamber parliament established in the reform of 1906 could not use them. Finland's becoming a sovereign power in 1917–1918 did not affect the single-chamber parliament, except that it gained parliamentary control of the executive power as regards government.

A fairly small steam vessel in the Saimaa Canal, at the Pälli lock. Passenger vessels, wooden "tar steamers" and barges in tow went through the Canal.

Tampere grew to be the centre of Finnish industry: the picture shows its textile factory in 1876.

After the Napoleonic Wars, the Russian hegemony ruled the Baltic area. Sweden and Denmark had lost their importance in major politics, Poland was no longer an independent state, Finland's annexation to the Russian Empire brought a Russian fleet and coastal garrisons all along the shores of the Finnish Gulf and the Gulf of Bothnia, and the very imposing fortifications of Bomarsund were built on the Åland Islands.

On the southern coast of the Baltic was the kingdom of Prussia, which became more powerful in the 19th century and finally in 1871 achieved the unification of Germany as an Empire under the leadership of Prussia.

Russia and Prussia were allies throughout almost the whole of the 19th century. They were bound by dynastic ties and by two important political interests. Together with Austria they guaranteed the decisions of the Vienna Congress 1814-1815, the object of which was to prevent a renewal of the French Revolution and other revolutions in Europe. Russia, Prussia and Austria were large, mainly agricultural countries, where the middle class did not yet have the political, industrial, commercial and intellectual status that they had achieved in France, England, Belgium and elsewhere more to the west. Moreover, the problems of the industrial workers and the big city proletariat were not yet felt in Eastern and Mid-Europe to the same extent as in Paris and London.

Russia, Prussia and Austria were especially bound by a joint policy regarding Poland: the desire to keep Poland divided between these three states. In the Polish rebellions in 1831 and par-

T'en as des ??... lèvres !

A postcard picturing the Russian - French military alliance, mailed from Algeria. The military alliance was of great significance from Finland's standpoint, because it defined Germany as the opponent, and this again made the question of Finnish coastal defence and of Finnish liability to military service topical.

ticularly in 1863, Prussia closed the frontier, and thus enabled Russia to put down the rebellions.

The Russian and Prussian alliance guaranteed a long-term peace in the Baltic area, broken off indeed by the Crimean War 1854-1856. Then the fleets of France and England sailed into the Baltic, destroyed Bomarsund, burned coastal cities of the Bothnian Gulf and the Finnish mercantile navy, and bombarded Sveaborg (Suomenlinna) off Helsinki. The main theatre of war was the Black Sea, but the Allies wanted to tie down Russian forces by threatening the vicinity of St. Petersburg.

In the 1880s the relations of Russia and Germany became strained, and in the early 1890s Russia and France approached each other, concluding a military alliance in 1893, aimed against Germany. The French-Russian alliance lasted to the end of World War I.

At the end of the 1890s Germany began a big naval shipbuilding programme; the main naval port was Kiel on the Baltic coast. Russia also started to build big warships for its Baltic fleet. At the same time it prepared for a possible German landing on the long coasts of the Baltic and Finland, from which it was a comparatively short distance to St. Petersburg.

The Finns had shown their loyalty to Russia during the Crimean War. In the war with Turkey 1877-1878 the Finns had also been on the side of Russia against Turkey and for the Balkan Christians, both in opinion and in the theatre of war. This loyalty led to the establishing of Finland's own military service army in 1878. The Finnish military burden was, however, considerably lighter than elsewhere in the Russian Empire.

In the new constellation envisaged in the 1890s, the potential enemy was not, however, faraway Turkey, but Germany, important intellectually, scientifically and industrially, and also close, and its possible ally Sweden-Norway.

Since the increasing of the military service burden caused great difficulties in Finland and aroused political agitation for several years, the separate Finnish army was discontinued. The task of defending the Grand Duchy of Finland remained entirely the responsibility of the Russian army, and Finland was obliged to pay considerably annual compensation in money instead of military service. Even during World War I the Finns were not mobilized. On the one hand Finnish political loyalty was no longer completely trusted, on the other hand Finland was an important supplier of war material.

In the final stages of World War I, Germany did, however, occupy the Baltic countries. During the Finnish War of Independence – Civil War a German Baltic division landed on the south coast of Finland at the beginning of April 1918, and defeated the Red government which had come into power in Helsinki at the end of January. Finland became a country closely bound to imperial Germany, but the defeat of Germany in autumn 1918 put an end to this relation.

In the 1920s France tried to form a pro-French alliance around Poland behind Germany's back. But Finland did not join in, though the project was in the air for a long time. In 1935 France and Russia (the Soviet Union) concluded a new military alliance, which however faded in August 1939, when Germany and the Soviet Union made the Ribbentrop-Molotov treaty, which meant the dividing of Poland and the defining of interests in the Baltic zone.

The Crimean War of the Turks and western powers against Russia in the 1850s was waged on two fronts, the Black Sea and the Baltic. A British-French fleet caused much damage on the Finnish coasts, destroyed almost all the Finnish mercantile fleet and the great fortress of Bomarsund in the Åland Islands, and also bombarded Sveaborg and Helsinki. The picture shows the bombardment of Sveaborg. The Finns remained loyal to Russia.

create a separate Finnish culture since this would serve to insulate the Finns from the Swedes. It would follow that, if Sweden tried to regain control of Finland, the Finns would not join the Swedes but would defend themselves and in so doing defend the Empire. During the Crimean War in the 1850's Sweden did in fact come close to allying itself to England and France, who were active in the Baltic Sea and bombarding the coast of Finland. With the exception of a few liberal students the Finns demonstrated their solidarity with Russia in this situation. Nicholas I (whose reign is so often considered to have represented a period of reaction) had no reason, for example, to prevent the birth of the Society of Finnish Literature in 1831. It was during Nicholas' reign, in fact, that first a Finnish language lectureship (1828) and later a professorship (1850) were established at the University, and this was at a time when new posts for lecturers in languages and particularly for professors were very rare indeed at universities anywhere. In the 1840's it began to be required that Finnish civil servants show proof of their command of the Finnish language and, in 1863, Czar Alexander II made Finnish an official language of administration and legal proceedings. In 1850, on the other hand, in order to prevent the circulation of political literature following the year of revolution in Europe (1848–49), the government placed a temporary restriction on publications in Finnish. The use of Finnish as a language of administration developed at the same

It is reckoned that the Finnish political press began with the publishing of the Saima newspaper by the philosopher J.V. Snellman; later Snellman edited other papers. He championed the cause of broad social participation (democracy), and thus acted to the benefit of the status of the Finnish language and culture, but the cultural language up to the end of the 19th century was almost solely Swedish. Swedish was also the language of Snellman, Runeberg and other Finnish-minded men. According to the constitutions of 1919 and 2000, the national languages of Finland are Finnish and Swedish.

time as the rise of a Finnish literary culture. Thus the press, on both languages, took on importance only in connection with the liberal breakthrough of the 1860's. The lack of intellectual resources in Finland and not a conservative government policy, therefore, was the main obstacle to the growth of a Finnish-language culture. All in all the educated class was rather small, which meant that it took a long time before they were able to create anything of a durable nature. This was true of both language groups. In Finland there were not, in fact, two distinct cultures, one Finnish-speaking and one Swedish-speaking: as far as output was concerned both cultures were essentially the same. The Finnish-speaking culture had long been dependent on the Swedish but, in terms of ideology, the Swedish-speaking culture was just as Finnish as the Finnish one itself. This ideology had been created by Runeberg, Lönnrot, Fredrik Cygnaeus, Snellman, Topelius and their contemporaries. Such figures as Yrjö-Koskinen and Julius Krohn (Suonio), who were responsible for much of the Finnish-speaking culture, had been brought up in Swedish-speaking and sometimes German-speaking environments. Many

members of the educated class began quite voluntarily to use Finnish. The transition from one cultural language to another took place relatively slowly and smoothly. Generally speaking the question of language placed no national or social limits on the bilingual educated class. The bilingual tradition has been very strong in Finland and its culture, lasting at least until the second World War, and is still, of course, very important today. This tradition has also kept Finland in close touch with the culture of Scandinavia. On the whole, the views on the position of the different languages were in close relation to the

opinions about how desirable the participation of wide circles in social activities was.

The formation of interest groups into political parties, a process which had begun in the 1860's, was partly the result of disputes over the position of the languages. The national and social programme of the Fennoman Party, in particular (the party was led by Professor G. Z. Forsman, who wrote under the name of Yrjö Koskinen and was later elevated to the ranks of the nobility and given the title Baron Yrjö-Koskinen) was closely linked with demands for improvements in the position of the Finnish language,

Fanny Churberg was an early, powerful woman artist who sought her themes from the drama of nature. The work is called Winter Road on Ice.

culture and economy. But, here too, what was involved was an entire programme which can be said to have represented, for the most part, the values and interests of the rural population, put forward in a spirit of national idealism and a kind of social conservatism. At this time the party was not an organization as such but consisted of a group of interests, supporting certain opinions, whose ranks included the majority of the clergy and the peasantry in the Diet, Finnish Clubs and Societies in many towns,

almost the entire Finnish press, which was expanding rapidly at the time, and a good half of the student bodies, especially those representing the inland areas. In the 1890's the Fennoman Party was split into two when a nationalist-liberal faction of "Young Finns" with the daily newspaper *Päivälehti* (1889, *Helsingin Sanomat* since 1904) as its spearhead, set themselves in opposition to the "Old Finns" led by Yrjö-Koskinen and the newspaper *Uusi Suometar.*

The other party grouping comprised the majority

In the 1880s the Helsinki Esplanade became a Parisian-style smart street. The Esplanade was originally a "fire wall" separating the part of the city built of stone from that of wood. An outdoor restaurant and the city's first theatre were built there, and later Helsinki's finest hotel. In the centre of the park avenue the city's first big public monument was erected, a statue of the national poet Runeberg.

The unveiling of the memorial statue of Emperor Alexander II in the Helsinki Senate Square in 1894. In front of the statue is the Maid of Finland, dressed in a bearskin, with her Lex shield and lion of Finland. The statue suggests Finland's favourable status in the Russian Empire; it has stood there ever since.

ard of living between those who owned forests and those who did not, with the latter losing their rights to the use of forest land. Rural conditions and the distribution of wealth were particularly affected by modernizations in agriculture – the development of methods of cultivation and cattle raising requiring greater capital outlay and producing larger profits. Cheap imported grain led to the domestic market concentrating on cattle farming and the exporting of butter. Farmers were able to increase their standard of living manyfold, renew their building stock, educate their children and purchase modern farming equipment, but only small changes were brought about in the conditions of the landless population and the difference between their standard of living and that of the landowners increased rapidly. The landless population comprised cottagers, who lived in rented cottages but had no land of their own, hired farmhands, who lived in and were dependent on the farm houses, as well as tenant farmers, who rented farmland but were obliged to work for the landowner when he so required. A great many of the rural population (their numbers had grown considerably throughout the century) moved to the towns to work in industry or emigrated. It was the rural proletariat which suffered most during the years of crop-failures and particularly during the famine of 1867–68. There was an awareness that reforms were necessary to improve the conditions of the rural landless, but changes did not occur. In the first Parliamentary elec-

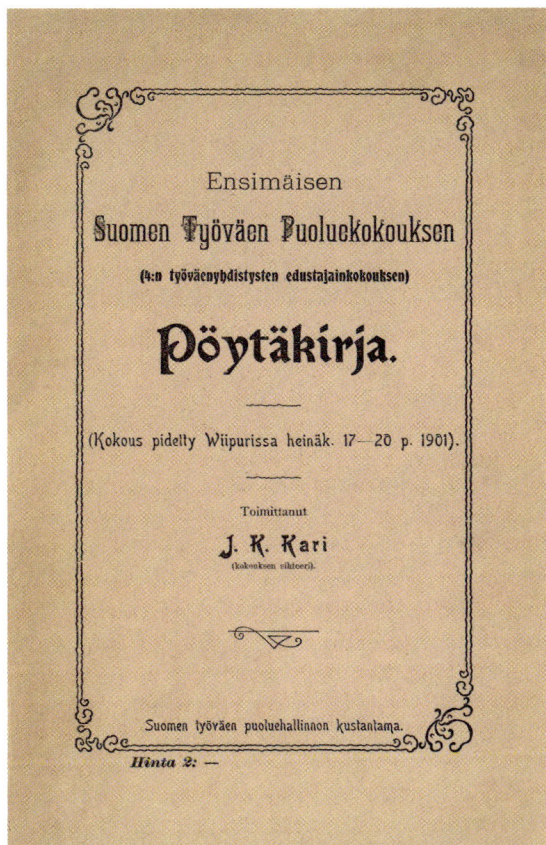

Ensimäisen
Suomen Työväen Puoluekokouksen
(4:n työväenyhdistysten edustajainkokouksen)

Pöytäkirja.

(Kokous pidetty Wiipurissa heinäk. 17—20 p. 1901).

Toimittanut
J. K. Kari
(kokouksen sihteeri).

Suomen työväen puoluehallinnon kustantama.

Hinta 2: —

The workers' societies developed into the workers' party and then the Social Democrat party. At an early stage country-wide meetings of members were held, and the minutes of their meetings were printed. The workers' movement had already achieved an established position when the general strike of 1905 broke out; this rapidly increased the significance and extent of the movement, and in 1907 led to a big election victory in the first universal suffrage elections.

tions to embrace universal suffrage in 1907 it was the rural proletariat that guaranteed the enormous success of the radical Social Democratic Party. However, in the face of opposition from the Czar and the government, Parliament could not put all the reforms it wished - like an alcohol prohibition law - into effect, a situation which led to the social tension that was an important feature in Finland at the turn of the century.

Along with tension on the domestic front came increased tension between Finland and Russia. The growing power of the German state led to a military alliance between Russia and France at the beginning of the 1890's and the strategic importance of Finland's south coast became greater. While improvements in Finland's defence and system of railways were undertaken to meet the changing situation, Russia began increasingly to doubt whether the Finnish people were still as loyal and trustworthy as they had been throughout the 19th century. In purely commercial terms Finland had already formed such strong ties with the West that her ties with Russia might be called into question, and strong cultural development was drawing Finland closer to Germany than to Russia. Russia made attempts to bring Finland more firmly back into its sphere of influence particularly in important military areas. But this led to conflict between the Russian government and the upper strata of Finnish society.

In 1898 the determined Russian General Nikolai

In the latter part of the 19th century, in the era of railways and newspapers, it was no longer sufficient for peoples and states to identify in the traditional military manner with ruling families, nor romantically with folk poetry, the Middle Ages or landscapes. More concrete and economic knowledge was required. To satisfy this need an enormous quantity of non-fiction writing, illustrated journals and photographs appeared, along with a series of big industrial and art exhibitions. Expressions of the same spirit of the times were also evident in international scientific congresses and exhibitions connected with them.

The first big world fairs were held in London in 1851 and 1862, and before this there were small agricultural and industrial exhibitions everywhere. The later London fair aroused interest in Finland as elsewhere, and two of the six Finnish exhibitors won gold medals. In fact Finnish participation in international fairs began at the Moscow Agricultural and Industrial Fair in 1864, the Stockholm Industrial Fair in 1866, and the Paris World Fair in 1867. The world fairs in Paris in 1889 and 1900 were especially important – as was Finland's own first big industrial fair in 1876.

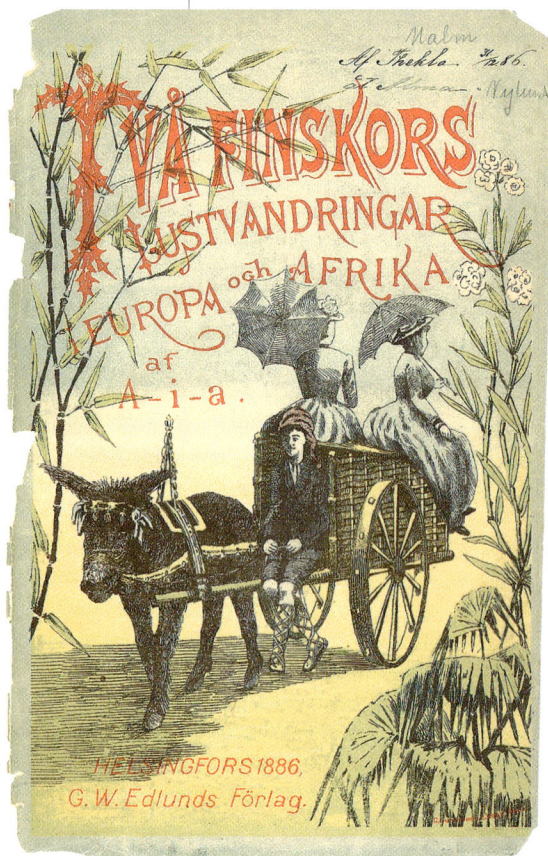

"The Pleasure Tours of Two Finnish Women" (1886) is a book (in Swedish) stressing women's independence and boldness in travelling both in Europe and Africa.

Besides exhibiting industrial products, every country had to consider what kind of general image of the country they wished to convey abroad. Both Sweden-Norway and Russia resorted largely to an ethnic-historical framework. In Finland at an early stage there arose a dispute between the ethnographic national presentation favoured by the Fennomanes, and the modern progressiveness of the Liberals. In addition another question became gradually more topical, of how to emphasize Finland's difference in the frame of the Russian Empire. Finland appeared abroad of course in connection with Russia.

In 1878 at the Paris World Fair Finland did not have its own stand, but later it did. In 1889 the relation with Russia did not cause a problem, as Russia did not wish to take part in a world fair arranged in honour of the centenary of the French Revolution. In 1900 the situation was more difficult, but was well arranged with the help of French conciliation. Finland had its own small pavilion, which aroused attention thanks to its architecture, its works of art and industrial products. Finland emphasized its press and telephone system, the importance of the folk school, its icebreakers and its art works – both the Kalevala world of Gallén and the refined sensualist sculpture of Vallgren. Music was also sent to the world fairs, primarily student choirs. In

1900 the most important representative of the "new school", Jean Sibelius, himself took part as an assistant conductor.

In connection with the world fairs, catalogues and general works of information presenting Finland were also made. Among the more ambitious of these were the extensive *Finland in the XIX Century* and *Atlas de Finlande* in the 1890s. The former was a multi-language publication, a splendidly illustrated general presentation of Finnish geography, history, education, science, art, industry and agriculture. The latter was described as the world's first "national atlas", with a diversity of maps illustrating the conditions and development of the country. The statistics section included not only the geography, geology and archaeology, but also the fields of research in which Finnish scientists had already at an early stage participated in international congresses and fairs.

Albert Edelfelt's well-known portrait of Pasteur shows in its own way how Finland belonged to the general European cultural world before World War I.

Madame Paris receives the little girl Helsinki at the World Exhibition in 1889: the letters E.U. stand for Exposition Universelle. At this Exhibition Finland emphasized its own special quality, and its definition vis-à-vis Russia caused disputes. In 1900 especially the Finnish pavilion and Finnish art aroused significant political attention; in the background was the constitutional dissension between Russia and Finland which had just arisen.

Finnish sea and inland shores and lighthouses according to the large Finnish Atlas published in 1910. The
Atlas also appeared in French.

The personification of Finland as a young maiden was developed in the late 19th century; sometimes she was dressed in a bearskin; here she is seen against the background of the ideal landscape of the interior. The Finnish blue and white colours were at first generally shown as two fields of colour, but in this postcard series printed in Sweden at the beginning of the 20th century the colours had already begun to form a cross in the Scandinavian fashion.

Ivanovich Bobrikov became Governor-General of Finland. The Manifesto of February, 1899 expressed an attempt to bring Finland back to the Russian fold. Faced with this situation, leading circles in Finland, particularly the alliance between the Swedish-minded Liberals and the "Young" Fennomen, which later formed the basis of the Constitutional of Opposition group, began to put up a concerted opposition. By making appeals to humanitarian and legal circles and by publicizing the achievements of Finnish culture and industry at such venues as the Paris World Fair in 1900, a great deal of attention was drawn to the Finnish question in Scandinavia, Germany and the

A very radical reform was made in Finland in 1906, when the Emperor and the Estates by general agreement implemented a single-chamber system and universal suffrage, the first in the world to include women's complete right to vote and eligibility for election. In the picture an election poster for the first elections in 1907. The Social Democrats surprisingly won 40% of the votes. The proportion of Socialists and women's right to vote were exceptional compared with other countries; this applied especially to the Russian Empire, to which Finland after all belonged.

Finnish women were the first in the world to obtain the right to vote and eligibility for office, when Emperor Nicholas I granted the Grand Duchy of Finland a new election law and a new Act of Parliament on June 20, 1906. The women's franchise was part of a big reform rescinding the Four Estates Diet and replacing it with a single-chamber parliament with 200 members, elected every three years by universal and equal vote. Every man and woman (with a few exceptions) of 24 years or more had the right to vote and also eligibility for office. The first elections according to this law were held in March 1907; 18 women were then also elected to the new Parliament.

Before the general franchise only about 15% of Finns had the right to vote. In the Estate of Burgesses women had had partial franchise based on wealth, but not eligibility for office. In local elections a "censitaire" right to vote was retained according to wealth and the census up to 1917.

Politicians of the new single-chamber parliament became at first a popular theme for caricaturists. It remained undecided whether the sounds of the various instruments would produce harmony or cacophony.

Women's political franchise was defended in Parliament, and women's position was not one of the main questions in the franchise debate, but was included in the extension of the right to vote generally. The Liberals and the Socialists supported women's franchise for reasons of principle; from the Conservative standpoint women represented values to be preserved in society, and on the whole the general and women's franchise were considered to reinforce Finland's special status as a Grand Duchy in the Russian Empire. A little before the Finnish parliamentary reform, Russia had, by the decision of the ruler, established a lower chamber, the *duma*, whose members were elected by the people of the whole empire. Only Finland was allowed to keep and reform its old separate representational system, although at first Finland too was directed to be part of the duma system.

The reform of the Russian and Finnish representational systems stemmed from the big phase of agitation in the Empire because of the lost war against Japan. The general state of unrest led to extensive strikes in 1905, first in Russia and then in Finland; the situation drifted almost to revolution, which the Empire managed, however, to avoid by concessions and by police action. The reform of the Finnish Four Estates system had already been planned, but the radicalization of the political situation forced the elite of the country and then the Emperor to agree to a general franchise. A large segment of the political field demanded the sum-

Alexandra Gripenberg.   Lucina Hagman.   Wuolijoki.   Schybergson.   Sirola.

Maria Laine.   Castrén.   Huoponen.   von Alfthan.   Danielson-Kalmari.

moning of the National Assembly prescribing the constitution, but the line representing continuity was victorious; according to this line a considerable reform was agreed in all four estates, and could be presented to the ruler as the aim of the assembly of the estates.

The single-chamber reform and the franchise reform did not, however, change the relative power of monarch and parliament. The ruler indeed dissolved the Parliament several times before the end of its term, but always ordered new elections immediately. Thus parliamentary elections were held in Finland in the middle of World War I in 1916; the Social Democrats gained a majority, a very unusual occurrence within the Russian Empire. They lost this position in new elections in 1917.

Finland's development in the latter part of the 19th century had already led to women being drawn into many social functions. In the lead were women's traditional roles as teachers and nurses, and training for these vocations was stepped up. In addition, there were many lower-level jobs in public administration, in the service of the post and telegraph offices, the railways and the like, and office work in private enterprise. A state system of girls' schools and private mixed schools appeared in Finland, and at the time of the first parliamentary elections one third of the students at the country's

Young people on a rowing trip at the beginning of the 20th century: students, both male and female, always wore the white student cap in summer.

single, large University were women, with the number constantly increasing. Foreign observers around 1900 considered women's independent and free status a special feature of Finland, although of course this did not yet affect all spheres of the community. In literature and painting women had at an early stage a conspicuous position.

Women's societies also played their own part as circulators of ideas about emancipation from abroad, but it may be generally said that women's emancipation received from the start much support and encouragement from the leading spheres of the society in Finland.

There was a woman minister in the Social Democrat minority government 1927-1928; this was an extremely early world-wide phenomenon. Later women ministers have become a normal feature in Finland, and in 1990 a Finnish woman was the first in the world to

hold the post of minister of defence.

In the 1960s and 1970s there came a new breakthrough for women who had started out on their studies and careers. The expanding society needed their contribution, the ideological trends of the time supported it, and social support for families, especially children's day care, was strikingly increased. Women of this age bracket then took over even the highest state positions in the 1990s; in 2001 a woman was elected for the first time to be President of Finland. In the academic world the proportion of women has also grown vigorously, but their share in business has remained distinctly smaller.

Veljeksillä POPOFF:

Varastossa vanhoa hyviksi tunnetuita Viiniä,
Kauppahuoneelta

S. LARCHER, JEUNE, BORDEAUX

sekä

Pariisin näyttelyssä vuonna 1889 palkittua **Punssia.**

HEDELMIÄ, tuoreita, | **HEDELMIÄ, säilytettyjä,**
ranskalaisia, saksalaisia, espanjalaisia, | sisäänpantuja, kuivattuja ja puristettuja,
italialaisia ja venäläisiä. | niinhyvin eurooppalaisia kuin aasialaisia.

T E E T A originaalipaketissa, parailta venäläisiltä kauppahuoneilta.

Chocolaadia,

ranskalaista Louit' Fieres'in, holantilaista Van Houtenin (Puhdasta cacaota), sekä
venäläistä uselta etevältä kauppahuoneilta.

Biscuits, suuri valikoima, seki englantilaista että venäläistä.

CONFITURES,

niinkuin chocolaadikonfektia, drageeta, karamellia, monpensieria ja marmelaadia.

Kuorimantelia, pistacioita ja useanlaisia pähkinöitä.

Conserveja, | **Juustoa,**
ranskalaisia, englantilaisia, saksalaisia, | ranskalaista, englantilaista, sveitsiläistä,
ruotsalaisia, venäläisiä ja kotimaisia. | venäläistä ja kotimaista.

☛ Erittäin hienoa Kuningas-Silliä. ☚

Siirtomaan-tavaroita,

kaikellaisia, rikas valikoima, priima laatua.

Paljottain ostettaessa myönnetään jälleenmyyjille edullinen alennus.

T I L A U K S I A

linnun, tuoreen kalan, kasviksien j. n. e. vastaanotetaan ja toimitetaan nopeaan ja
huokeasta.

VELJEKSET POPOFF,

P. Esplanadink. 27 ja Kluuvikatu 1.

Goods from various parts of Europe and Asia could be obtained from Helsinki commercial firms, some of which at least had come via St. Petersburg. The picture is from 1889.

western world in general. At home, public opinion was organized on a wider basis with the collection and presentation to the Czar of a "Grand Petition" signed by half a million Finns and especially by opposition to a law designed to conscript Finns into the Russian army. There were deep differences of opinion, however, as to what attitude should be taken to Russian aims. The "Old" Fennomen, in particular, favoured a strategy of negotiations aimed, primarily, at keeping the Senate and the administrative machinery in Finnish hands. The opposition, the Constitutionalists, saw this as following a line of submission. The "Old" Fennomen became embittered at doubts thrown on their patriotism for remaining in the Senate when their opponents resigned. Bobrikov's period, which is known emotionally as the "years of oppression", came to an end with his assassination in summer 1904 and to a political conclusion with the general strike of autumn 1905.

The political plane of Finland's internal situation and relation with Russia during the government of Nicholas II was coloured by conflicts. But as regards economic, scientific and artistic matters it was a successful period - a real "Golden Age".

With Russia losing the war with Japan and the Czar obliged to agree to the establishment of a system of popular representation in Russia, the government's policy towards Finland underwent a change. In Finland, the old Four-Estates Diet was replaced by a single-chamber Parliament in 1906. At a stroke Fin-

Heino Aspelin's caricature of Sibelius in 1904. Jean Sibelius composed his important works in the first quarter of the 20th century, and was already famous before World War I. Sibelius's style developed from art nouveau romanticism to classicism; he combined Finland's popular (Finnish-language) and cultural (Swedish-language) traditions, together with Russian and German influences in his personal life's work. His world fame had an influence compared with that of the Kalevala in the previous century. Together with Mannerheim he became the most famous Finn of all time.

The fifth symphony, the themes of the four-part original project in tabular form. On 29 July 1914 Sibelius wrote in his diary: "War declared. Austria - Serbia." On the same day he had "been given" a delightful theme which he was "hammering out"; he had started work on his fifth symphony. Sibelius performed "his newest works", including the fifth symphony, on his fiftieth birthday, 8 December 1915. The World War did not then affect Finland directly, but there were many Russian troops in Finland awaiting a possible landing by Germany. The war came to Finland with much bloodshed in spring 1918, when Germans and Russians also fought in the Finnish war between Whites and Reds.

The office building of the Helsinki Telephone Association designed by Lars Sonck represents the interest in raw granite facades that prevailed in Helsinki architecture for some time. The building is a reminder also of the early growth of telephonic communication in Finland.

land changed over from the oldest parliamentary system in Europe to the most modern. Under universal suffrage the number of voters in the country increased tenfold and Finland became the first country in Europe to extend the franchise to women. In the elections which followed, the Social Democratic Party, in which revolutionary views held an important position, gained 40 % of the mandate, its share increasing in subsequent elections until, in 1916, the socialists gained a majority in Parliament. Following the general strike and a shift in government policy in Russia, decrees enacted in Bobrikov's time were repealed and a Senate led by Mechelin came into power. Despite its reform, the new Parliament had no constitutional basis which meant that the Senate and the Governor-General were dependent on the confidence of the Czar. In 1909, as the political situation changed, first the Constitutionalists and later the "Old" Fennomen resigned from the Senate their place being taken by pro-government civil-servants who lacked the confidence of Parliament and the political parties, and from 1912 onwards, under a law giving equal status to Finnish and Russian subjects, by native Russians too. Finland's Governor-General from 1909 until the Revolution was General F. A. Seyn, who was given the task of preventing the re-occurrence of such events as the general strike of 1905 and of thwarting Finnish and Russian revolutionary activities. This period of Finnish history is known as the second period of oppression but eco-

Jugend-style houses at the beginning of the 20th century. The corner buildings are dwelling houses designed by Eliel Saarinen who is better known for his monumental works.

Finnish success in the Stockholm Olympic Games of 1912 increased national self-confidence, although Finland could not appear as a completely independent nation. In the picture Hannes Kolehmainen beats the Frenchman Jean Bouin in the 5 000 metres event.

nomically and culturally it was a fruitful time in many respects. It was also a time which saw, in addition to the growing tension in Finnish-Russian relations, a widening gap between bourgeois and socialist social groups. Under these conditions there was a growing desire, especially in Swedish-speaking quarters, to seek links with Sweden and, upon the outbreak of the first World War, with Germany. These aims are reflected in the fact that during the World War many young Finnish men volunteered to join not only the Russian army but also left to train as infantrymen in the army of the enemy, Germany, and that, following the war, White Finland (the country was divided into White and Red camps) formed close contacts with the still fairly strong Imperial Germany.

INDEPENDENT FINLAND

The Russian Revolution of March 1917 restored Finland to a position of autonomy. As the spring progressed, however, many Finns advanced the idea of complete independence from Russia while still more were of the opinion that Finland's future lay in the same kind of autonomous position that it had held under Russia in the 19th century. Those in favour of separation included, for the most part, the left-wing

The Helsinki Railway Station, completed in 1914, reveals Finland's wealth and advanced development. The Finnish railway network still follows the Russian width of track. The entrance to the Emperor's waiting salon can be seen in the picture; Emperor Nicholas II only once managed to use it. Later this door has been used for the reception of Soviet-Russian heads of state. Swedish, Danish and Estonian heads of state have traditionally arrived by ship, and today of course generally by air. In the foreground there are buses.

Lenin's Soviet-Russia acknowledged Finland's sovereignty on 4 January 1918, and Sweden, Germany and France followed immediately, as did most other European countries. Great Britain and The United States did not acknowledge Finland's independence until over a year later, because they considered that Finland had moved into the sphere of influence of Imperial Germany – which was in fact true. Finland was actually the first of the new states born as a result of World War I, but it already had an old existence as a state, even if not a sovereign one. In a caricature Lenin puts the French bonnet of liberty on the head of the Maid of Finland, with the help of the Swedish king and the German emperor.

and the pro-German section of the bourgeoisie. In summer 1917, the Finnish Parliament assumed the power that had been vested in the Czar but the Russian Provisional Government under Alexander Kerenski, dissolved the Finnish Parliament and the enabling Act lapsed. These events widened the gap between the bourgeoisie and the left who had pushed through the Act. In the autumn elections the balance of power in Parliament changed with the bourgeoisie gaining a majority and Parliament decided once more to "assume authority" since attitudes towards Russia in bourgeois circles had been changed once and for all by the October Revolution. The so-called Independence Senate, led by P. E. Svinhufvud, proclaimed Finland an independent republic on 4 December 1917, and this was approved by Parliament on 6 December 1917. Foreign powers were unwilling to recognize Finnish independence before the Soviet government had done so. On 31 December 1917, upon the request of the Senate, Lenin's government announced its recognition of the new state, after which France, Sweden, Germany, Austro-Hungary, Greece, Norway and Denmark quickly followed suit; Great Britain and the United States, on the other hand, recognized Finland's independence only one and a half years later. Recognition of Finnish independence, however, did not mean the withdrawal of Soviet troops stationed in Finland in spite of attempts by the Finnish Senate to accomplish this.

The socialists were no longer so eager to break

From the start in 1918 Mannerheim became a legendary figure to "White Finland" as well as abroad, but in the 1930s he gradually gained the respect of the whole nation both for his humanitarian activities and his pronouncements emphasizing national unanimity. Mannerheim represented the Scandinavian tendency dear to the Social Democrats also as opposed to the ardent Finnish and extreme right-wing spirit. When the Winter War started he had to take over the position of Commander-in-Chief in spite of his doubts and age, and his authority in the years that followed was an extremely important factor in holding together the nation and the army. In the postcard he is shown surrounded by Finland's historical coats-of-arms of the provinces.

In the new Finland born from the upheaval of 1917–1919, Mannerheim became the most conspicuous leader, first as General of the Whites in 1918, then in 1919 as Regent, later Field Marshal, Commander-in-Chief 1939–1945, Marshal of Finland from 1942, and President of Finland 1944–46. He was honoured in parades, national subscriptions, postage stamps and portraits. On his 75th birthday in 1942 something central in Helsinki and many other Finnish cities was given a new name after him; the same day Hitler, leader of the still victorious Germany, flew to Finland to congratulate him. At the end of the war the victors refrained from demanding that Mannerheim be put on trial. His funeral in 1951 was a noteworthy patriotic occasion, and the unveiling of his equestrian statue in 1960 was a ceremony that united the people in remembering the significance of the war and the contribution of those who took part in it. Abroad he was shown continued homage by the victorious states as well as others; a monument was erected in his honour on the shore of Lake Geneva.

As the first great military figure and statesman of newly-independent Finland, Mannerheim became the new object of the previously monarchic respect for the ruler. The older great men of Finland, especially Runeberg, Lönnrot and Snellman, were all men of the intellectual world. Mannerheim then came to embody statesmanship. He was excellently suited to this task through his appearance, behaviour, distinction, foreign connections and simple military dignity.

The respect and admiration accorded to Mannerheim by the Whites in 1918 were at first inevitably reversed in the attitude of the Reds. But gradually his policy of conciliation won appreciation. During the Winter War and the Continuation War the propaganda slander directed at Mannerheim's person by the Soviet Union evoked no response at all in Finland. On his birthday in 1942 Mannerheim received, to his great appreciation, congratulations from representatives of the Finnish workers. His significance as an architect of peace in 1944 and a guarantor that the peace agreement would be observed was broadly esteemed in various political spheres, including the Allies and even Stalin himself.

At times, especially in the 1970s, Mannerheim's person and significance were disparaged; this occurred in connection with efforts to re-evaluate the past and the choices made otherwise. But from the 1980s his prestige rose again; several biographies and studies about him have appeared again, and he is an object of considerable interest in Russia too. Because Mannerheim was for a long period an officer in the Emperor's Imperial Army, and a general who fought in the Japanese War and World War I, and because he was an important explorer, the events of his life before his vital contribution to Finnish history are also of dramatic interest.

An obelisk embellished with the imperial double-eagle was erected in the Helsinki Market Place in honour of the first visit to Finland of the Empress Alexandra in 1833. In 1917 Russian mariners dragged the double-eagle down, but it was put back in place in the 1960s.

with Russia. The radical left, hoping for a revolution in Finland too, achieved the ascendancy in the Social Democratic Party. At the end of January, 1918 the "Reds" took over power in Helsinki and southern Finland. The Senate fled to Vaasa in Ostrobothnia where they established a "White" stronghold controlling northern and central Finland. General Gustaf Mannerheim was called in to take control as commander-in-chief of the "White" forces and, at the beginning of April, he won the decisive battle for Tampere. At the same time, at the invitation of the Senate, a German division landed on the south coast of Finland, taking Helsinki and other towns. The role played by the Germans in supporting the "Whites" and that of Russia in supplying arms and assistance to the "Reds" is a clear indication of the fact that, in addition to Finland's internal affairs, the war also involved the question of the spheres of interest of the Major Powers. At the outbreak of the first World War Germany had already attempted to pave the way to rebellion in Finland by training a group of Finnish volunteers as light-infantrymen. With the end of the war in spring 1918, Germany made efforts to tie Finland firmly to its sphere of interest. At the political level this is seen from the fact that the Kaiser's brother-in-law, Prince Friedrich Karl of Hessen, was elected King of Finland. Germany's collapse prevented him from ever ascending the throne, however, and at the same time Finland was freed from its economic and military alliance with Germany. Mannerheim,

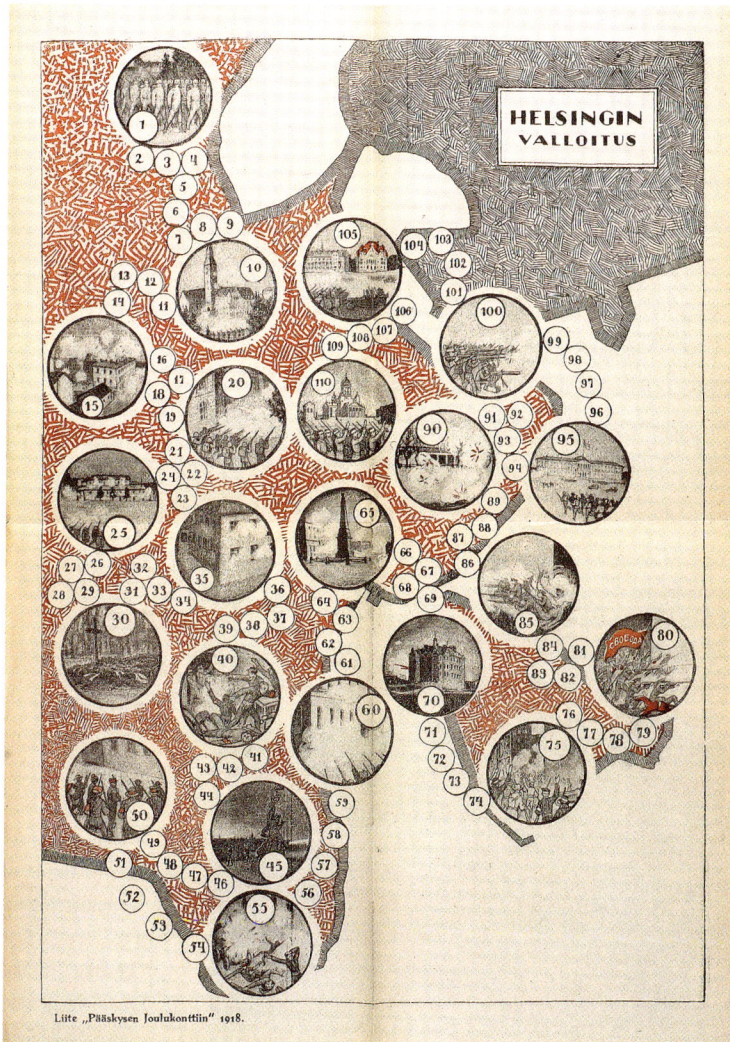

HELSINGIN VALLOITUS

Liite „Pääskysen Joulukonttiin" 1918.

The War of Independence-Civil War was the theme of many novels and plays, booklets concerning political and cultural issues, and also games; this game intended for children is built up on the various stages of the capturing of Helsinki in April 1918.

who had opposed the pro-German trend in Finland, became regent and under his leadership the country began to look towards the western world. On 17th July, 1919 the Constitution was ratified by Mannerheim and Finland's relations with foreign states were normalized. Under a peace treaty signed with Russia at Tartu (Dorpat) in 1920, the area of Petsamo in Lapland was added to Finland's former territory, which meant that the country now extended to the Arctic Ocean; Finland was later to lose this area under the armistice of 1944.

The Finnish Constitution was created as a compromise between republican and monarchist opinion. It left the President with most of the power enjoyed by the head of state under the previous constitution: responsibility for foreign policy, the position of Commander in Chief of the army and the right to dissolve Parliament. While the President's position within the system of state became of central importance, a multi-party system led to short-term governments varying in their political composition.

With the Constitution affording the President a central position in affairs of state, the first two Presidents of the Republic, K. J. Ståhlberg and L. Kr. Relander, both exercised their right to dissolve Parliament in the face of opposition from the Council of State. Neither did the next President, P. E. Svinhufvud adhere to the classical principles of democracy, with minority governments in power through most of his term of office. By contrast K. Kallio's term of

UUSI
EDUSKUNTATALO

LE NOUVEAU PALAIS
DE LA CHAMBRE DES
DÉPUTÉS DE FINLANDE

1931   DOMUS   1

in support for the Left in the years immediately following the war. With the exception of Tanner's minority Social Democratic government (1926–1927) the 1920's was a period of government by centre and right-wing coalitions. The 1930's was a time of "Presidential" governments (foremost among which was the long-lived Kivimäki administration) until 1937 when, with K. Kallio becoming President, a Social Democrat–Agrarian–Progressive Party coalition came into power.

The greatest change to take place in the form of government since independence, apart from the change-over from a hereditary monarchy to a regular-

The Parliament House completed in 1931 and designed by J.S. Sirén became the noble classical monument of the new Finnish Republic. It was thought that the area of this building and the National Museum would become the equivalent of the Senate Square which symbolized the Grand Duchy. The single-chamber parliament itself in fact dated back to the Grand Duchy; the fine Assembly house of the three non-noble Estates of the 1890s and the older House of the Nobility had become inconvenient. The new Parliament House was designed as a "work of overall art"; all the details of interior decoration and embellishment were part of the same ambitious plan. The classical trend otherwise produced several beautiful buildings.

Animal husbandry became a vitally important form of livelihood in the latter part of the 19th century, when cheap imported grain began to replace domestic grain cultivation with the improvement of the transportation. Finnish butter became an important export to Russia and Great Britain. Animal husbandry strengthened the status of women and brought them their own earnings.

ly elected head of state, was the adoption of Parliamentary principles. Otherwise Finland, unlike most other countries achieving independence after World War I, already had its own system of representation and administration, elections by universal suffrage, its own civil service and financial institution, its own economy and culture.

The political significance of the war of 1918 lies in the fact that it determined whether Finland would follow Russia on the road to revolution. In the anti-revolutionary sense, in removing Russian troops from Finland and securing the country's political independence, it was a "war of liberation" which came to a conclusion at Tarto in 1920. As a "civil war" its roots lay largely in the growing dissatisfaction with social inequalities that had long been smouldering beneath the surface. Soon after the war the reforms which had long been planned but which had been postponed because of political circumstances, were put into effect. The most important reform concerned the finding of land for the landless population and freeholds for tenant farmers.

During the early years of independence acts were passed introducing compulsory education, prohibition of alcohol (repealed in 1932), freedom of worship, freedom of speech and freedom to form societies. Legislation was introduced regulating the position of the two language groups and an Act was passed providing autonomy for the Åland Islands, an area over which Finnish sovereignty had been confirmed by the League of Nations and which had long represented a bone of contention between Finland and Sweden. During Ståhlberg's period as President, an Act of Amnesty was passed under which those convicted as leaders of the "Reds" were quickly pardoned in an attempt to dispel the destructive memories of the War in 1918. As early as in the spring of 1919, the Social Democratic Party, the representative of the losing side in the war, could participate in the elections and became the largest party in Parliament. By 1926 the Social Democrats alone formed the Government, a fact which can be seen as an indication of the stabilization of the democratic system. This success is explained in part by the fact that the Left had split in two, with the Social Democrats representing the moderate wing of the old Socialist Party. The revolutionary wing founded the Finnish Communist Party in the Soviet Union in 1918, but this was illegal in Finland until 1944. Otherwise the Agrarian Party and the Swedish Party continued as before with the Finnish-speaking section of the bourgeoisie reforming their ranks to fight over the constitutional form the country was to have. The monarchists formed the National Coalition Party, which was made up for the most part of members of the "Old" Fennoman Party, while the Republicans formed the Progressive Party around a core of "Young" Fennomen. In addition to two other small parties, the Christian Party and a political group which fronted for the Communists, another party to

emerge at this time was the Fascist-like Patriotic People's Movement (IKL). Founded in 1933, its early support soon dwindled and it was proscribed under the armistice of 1944.

In spite of many economic difficulties and a relatively low standard of living, a spirit of optimism prevailed in Finland throughout the 1920's, a mood which was heightened by the success of Finnish athletes, by the appearance of new literature, by the kind of international intercourse, with its diplomats and state visits, for which sovereignty is a prerequisite, and by Finland's participation in the League of Nations. On the other hand, the world-wide economic depression at the end of the decade led to difficulties in Finland too: bankruptcies, auctions of property and shortages. The language disputes, which had flared up once again, were a prominent issue throughout the 1920's and 1930's, but they did not lead to any legislation of note.

The great depression, which began at the end of the 1920's and continued until the middle of the next decade, was felt in Finland too, both financially and politically. Unemployment grew and in an agrarian country the fact that on a large scale smallholdings had such debts that they were forced to compulsory auctions was a disturbing phenomenon. Many banks were obliged to stop functioning or to merge with larger banks.

The social crisis naturally increased political pressures. Linked to this was the worry concerning the

The Finnish Opera (later the National Opera) obtained the building of the Russian Alexander Theatre on the Boulevard in Helsinki, and thus regular performances of opera and ballet began in Finland. Operas and especially operettas had indeed been performed a good deal on other stages previously. Now the first domestic ballet, Secrets of Happiness *appeared; this ensemble scene of white-dressed maidens is from that ballet. Finnish ballet tradition sprang from the directing of St. Petersburg ballet maestros.*

A colour picture in a humorous Christmas magazine in 1932 managed to include all the wonders of the times on a map of Finland: the new Parliament House, the rescinding of the Prohibition Law, the suppressing of the rightist Lapua Movement, the Olympic Games. On the shores of Lake Ladoga references to the area of the Orthodox monasteries and Russia can be seen.

spread of communism and the developments within the Soviet Union. The collectivization and the population transfers in the Soviet Union gave visible reason to fear changes. It was under such circumstances that the anti-communist Lapua movement was born and grew. The movement which gained wide support in 1930 at the time of the great peasants' march to Helsinki gradually became more radical, culminating in an attempt at an armed rebellion in spring 1932. The movement was part of a general European trend against liberalism and the parliamentarism of the 1920's: in place of the monetary power, moral degeneration which they represented, more state con-

TYÖVÄEN -
PUOLUE
VALTAAN!

ÄÄNESTÄ
SOSIALIDEMOKRAATTEJA

In 1936 the Social Democrats emphasized the workers' spirit but at the same time stressed parliamentarism by showing a picture of the new Parliament House; thus the party was not revolutionary but co-operative in spirit. In fact a centre–left-wing coalition government was formed in the following year, and the same combination determined the presidential election.

trol and planning were sought particularly so that new attempts at the failed leftist revolutions after the world war could be prevented. Although there had been an attempt at a left wing revolution in Finland in 1918, Finland preserved a parliamentary model throughout the 1932 situation and its after effects. This soon drew Finland closer to the other Nordic countries, since the Baltic countries and especially Germany were moving in the 1930 in various forms towards a one-party system and dictatorial power.

After 1932 in Finland too there was a movement to long-term governments. At first the government was weak as far as parliamentary support was concerned and it leant above all on the President (P. E. Svinhufvud). It stabilized the situation both politically and financially and began to move the emphasis of foreign policy away from the League of Nations towards the security system of the Nordic countries. In 1937, with a change in Presidents, the so-called "red-green" coalition was formed, in which the Agrarian Party and the Social Democrats began a long period of co-operation. As far as internal politics were concerned it meant the rejection of the 1918 division, agreement over the language disputes of the 1920's and 1930's, and the beginning of a social security system: as far as foreign policy was concerned it meant co-operation with the Swedish Social Democrat government and the rejection of the German alternative. The Foreign Ministers were Anglophiles, the government coalition resembled slightly the

Olli Miettinen's La Piste *(1931) demonstrates Parisian influences of the period.*

French example, and the general direction was towards the Nordic countries. Financial development and a rise in the standard of living also muffled the extreme right wing, and the fascist-like IKL Party which was born out of the Lapua movement was reduced to a minor factor. In military terms, however, Finland was oriented towards the West.

The general liberalizing tone of the thirties was expressed in the Anglo-saxon tone of the newspapers and films, whereas the stimulus for the pictorial arts and architecture came mostly from France. In place of Neo-Classicism came the Functionalist style with its predominance in building production, metal furniture and the Artek form based on the use of Finnish materials. In the field of philosophy and the "world view", empirism and the new trends in psychology, particularly freudism, received attention; the general trend in cultural life changed from the narrowly nationalistic to a more open attitude to Europe, and in the field of the natural sciences the influence of the United States began to be felt at the end of the decade.

In this optimistic atmosphere the threat of a great war did not lead to any considerable development in defensive preparedness in spite of the reports of Marshal Mannerheim, who had become chairman of the Defence Council at the beginning of the decade. When, therefore, the Soviet Union as early as 1938 secretly and in 1939 publicly demanded negotiations and exchanges of territory, Finland did not for a long

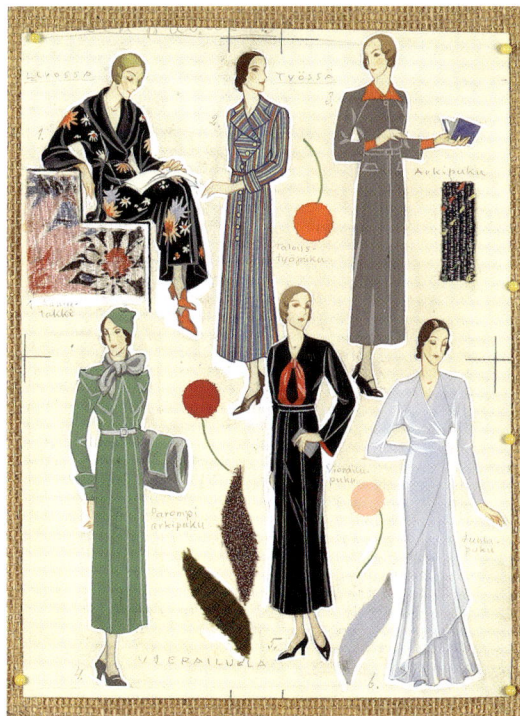

The illustrator Martta Wendelin also drew fashionable art; in 1933–1934 classical stylishness was emphasized.

time believe that the demands would lead to war. The Soviet Union's attack in November 1939 was to Finland and the world to a great extent a surprise.

The Soviet Union had that classic security problem: the need to shift the defence of Leningrad and north-west Russia back to the mouth of the Gulf of Finland, since on Finland's and Estonia's independence it had been obliged to draw the line very close to Leningrad. Finnish military connections with Ger-

Naistenlehdestä:

».... ja tähden jalkoja — Hollywoodin korkeimmin vakuutettuja — verhosivat seitinohuet sukat ...»

— Hm. Ovathan ne kauniit — kieltämättä — mutta hänenkaltaisellaan diivalla onkin varaa uhrata kokonaisia omaisuuksia tuollaisiin »hämähäkinseittimäisiin sukkiin. Sitä minulla valitettavasti ei ole ...

— Minäpä väitän, että kellä tahansa kontsorinaidillä on niin paljon varaa. SILVALLA pestyt silkkisukathan kestävät kokonaisen ikuisuuden ja tulevat joka pesussa vain kauniimmiksi.

vaahtoaa
kylmässäkin
vedessä

SILVA

VILLAN JA SILKIN YSTÄVÄ

HAVIN OSAKEYHTIO • VIIPURI

In this luxuriously care-free laundry ad of autumn 1939 the threat of war cannot yet be perceived at all. The country's most popular women's magazine Hearthside reflected the home and family ideals of agrarian – middle-class Finland, but its advertisements also reveal the presence of the super-womanly type mainly associated with the world of the American movies.

The Peace of Tartu (Dorpat) 1920 confirmed the old Russian border of the Grand Duchy of Finland as the new frontier, and this internal border of the old Russian Empire now became the boundary between two sovereign states. In addition, Finland was granted a corridor to the Arctic Ocean: the Petsamo area in Lapland. For many Finns it was a disappointment that Russian Karelia (Eastern Karelia) was not united with Finland. It had never been part of the Swedish kingdom, nor of the Grand Duchy of Finland; it belonged traditionally to the Orthodox Church and was partly Russian-speaking, but for folkloric, geographical and forest management reasons it had begun to be considered symbolically Finnish. The uniting of Eastern Karelia and Finland was a topical question all through the 1920s, when it was hoped that a referendum could be achieved through pressure from the League of Nations.

From Russia's standpoint, the conclusion of peace with Finland, the Baltic countries and Poland meant, on the other hand, the loss of former regional dominance in the Baltic, and also the exacerbation of St. Petersburg's classic security question, though it was agreed to destroy certain frontier fortifications. But at the Rapallo talks in 1922 the countries at whose cost the new small states had been created – Germany and the Soviet Union, sought support from one another. At Locarno in 1925 Germany became stronger by obtaining the support of the Western powers for its position. Russia and France then formed an alliance in 1935.

As early as 1935 the Soviet ambassador warned the Finns that leaving the security question of Leningrad undecided would be a *casus belli*. The Russians returned to the matter in 1938 with a direct

The Soviet Union thought they could easily beat the Finns when they launched their attack on 30 November 1939. Hitler and Stalin had just agreed that Finland belonged to the Soviet sphere of interest. But Finland succeeded in defending itself for three months of hard frost, destroying Soviet regiments unused to winter warfare and achieving an unprecedented spirit of national solidarity and will to defend. Since there were no other war operations going on at the time, the international press concentrated on Finland and sided with the Finns, and Winter War Finland won outstanding goodwill. On 13 March 1940 Finland, unconquered, concluded a difficult but honourable peace and preserved its independence.

proposal for exchanges of territory. Finland certainly did not give sufficient attention to this proposal, for the Soviet Union was primarily considered a country of international communism and, at that particular time, of terrorism, and thus a potential – but hardly a direct – threat to Finland.

Instead, Finland cultivated its relations with Germany – very conspicuously in that year, 1938 – by taking part in a twenty-years' commemoration of 1918, and at the same time military cooperation with Germany and Estonia were developed through naval manoeuvres and plans. Swedish

military headquarters showed great interest in defence cooperation with Finland. But since the noisy demands for expansion into Eastern Karelia by the Finnish Civil Guard and the student world that had earlier prevailed had quietened down and was modified to become defence propaganda

defence plan come about: the country was obliged to go to war alone and ill-equipped.

But the Soviets too had difficulties and inexperience particularly in respect of winter warfare, and the Finnish army – whose Commander in Chief had become Marshal Mannerheim – achieved several considerable victories in repelling attacks to begin with in the north, at Suomussalmi and Raate where the Red Army tried to push their way towards Oulu in order to cut Finland in two. It was, however, clear that Finland could not last long against an enemy of far greater power. When the Soviet Union gave up its support to the marionette government it had established on the Karelian Isthmus, an armistice was concluded in March 1940. The Finnish army had withdrawn to the gates of Viipuri (Vyborg) but the front held out until the end and partly guaranteed the preconditions for an honourable but heavy defeat. It realized the Soviet Union's original aims: a base in Hanko and the moving of the border further from Leningrad.

The area surrendered was about one tenth of Finland's area and the population slightly more: all Karelians thought it better to come to what was left of Finland than to remain in their home districts. In terms of those fallen and wounded Finland's losses in the Winter War had been great. The Winter War left the Finns with a feeling of injustice which was mitigated by the awareness that the result, the maintenance of sovereignty, was gained by unanimity and

resolution. These factors had an important effect in reorientation when relationships between the Soviet Union and Germany began to be strained. Germany began to show an interest in Finland and this was received in post-war Finland with a sense of relief, in a situation in which Soviet policy was understood in wide circles to be still anti-Finland. When Hitler attacked the Soviet Union in the summer of 1941 there were already German troops in northern Finland, which in fact became an area of German military operations. The situation in Northern Europe had undergone a drastic change by the incorporation of the Baltic Countries into the Soviet Union and the occupation of Denmark and Norway by Germany. German operations in northern Finland related, as a matter of fact, to Norway.

Finland did not, however, form an alliance with Germany, and both the Finnish government and the Commander in Chief followed strategy which served the purposes of Finland alone during the war. Thus Finland did not actively participate in the siege of Leningrad nor did it break Leningrad's service line to the Arctic Ocean. Mannerheim understood that Finland and the Soviet Union or Russia would still be neighbours even after the war. Finland did, however, occupy part of Eastern Karelia on the other side of the border. There were plans to annex this area to Finland. This was the area that Finland had tried to obtain in 1919–1920, and in 1939 the Soviet Union had offered this area to Finland as an exchange of

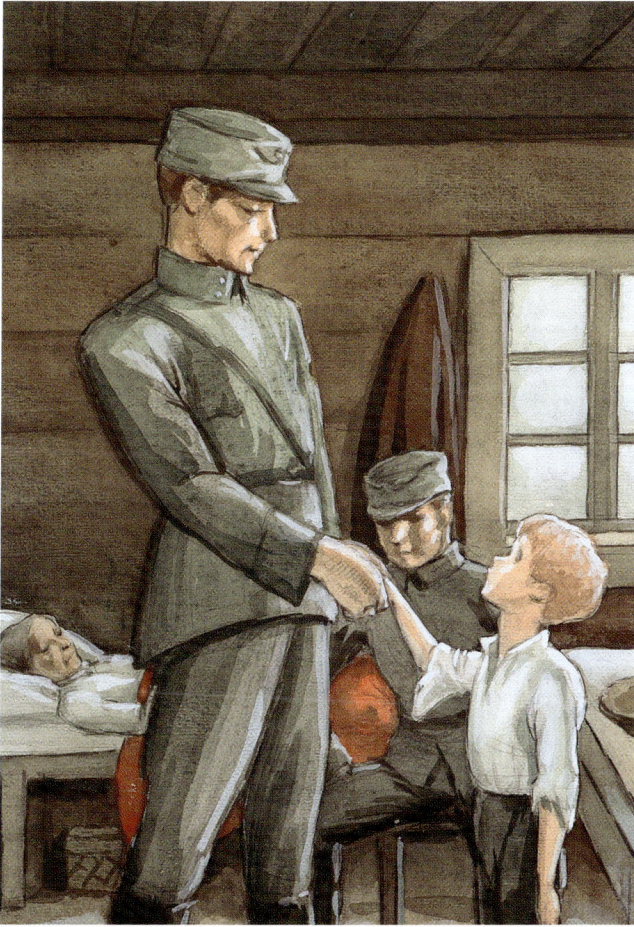

According to wartime propaganda, there was a great difference between the educational level and humanity of Finnish and Russian soldiers. Drawing by Rudolf Koivu.

Красноармейцы! Мы относимся ко всем военнопленным хорошо.

Согласно новому приказу Главного Командования Финской Армии, добровольно перешедшим на нашу сторону красноармейцам, предоставляются особые преимущества. Они получат лучшую пищу, лучшее помещение и желающим организуется подходящая работа.

Боец, решайся немедленно! При первом удобном случае переходи смело на нашу сторону.

Если не можешь сохранить эту листовку, то переходи без нее или оторви угол со штемпелем и бери с собой.

КОМАНДОВАНИЕ ФИНСКОЙ АРМИЕЙ
ГЛАВНОЕ

SUOMEN ARMEIJAN PÄÄLLYSTÖ

Tämän esittäjä siirtyy vapaaehtoisesti Suomen puolelle ja on häntä kohdeltava hyvin.

A Finnish propaganda leaflet addressed to Soviet soldiers, urging them to surrender. The text is in Russian, but for Finns there is a message that "the bearer of this leaflet is moving voluntarily to the Finnish side and he must be treated well."

The year 1944 was the most dramatic of the war. In February the Allies (Soviet Union) directed three big aircraft assaults primarily at Helsinki, but effective antiaircraft action prevented heavy destruction. Finland did not accede to the too severe terms offered for a separate peace, since its armies were still undefeated deep in East Karelia. In June a massive enemy attack on the Karelian Isthmus and to the north of Lake Ladoga was one of the biggest in World War II. It was the Soviet equivalent to the landing of the western Allies in Normandy at the same time, which attracted the attention of the whole world so that Finland's struggle was hardly recognized. The Finnish land forces were considerably smaller than those of the Soviet, and they did not have the tremendous armoured and aircraft equipment of the enemy. The artillery, however, managed to fight off the waves of assault, and then vital assistance was obtained from Germany in the form of aircraft and anti-tank equipment. The Red Army got as far as Viipuri, but was repulsed by storms of fire at Tienhaara, Tali and Ihantala, and the Soviet attack was halted in July. Finland agreed to a separate peace on slightly easier terms than in spring; an armistice and truce were concluded in September. In the picture the main building of the University burning in the Helsnki Senate Square with the monument of Alexander II a sad figure in the foreground.

territory and also annexed it to Finland with an agreement made that year by the puppet government. Essentially, however, it was a question of moving the war into the adversary's territory, of a tactical viewpoint and a potential territory for exchange during the making of peace.

From the year 1943 onwards Finland investigated the possibility of a separate peace but, on the one hand, the situation concerning supplies and the fear of a German occupation and, on the other hand, the harsh peace terms postponed the armistice until September 1944. In the spring 1944 there had been heavy bombing of particularly Helsinki and, during summer, extremely severe fighting on the Karelian Isthmus where the advance of enemy had been halted, on the one hand, at Vuoksi in the fierce battles of Taipale and, on the other hand, west of Viborg in the heavy battles of Tienhaara, Tali and Ihantala. At this point Finland made a pact with Germany and received significant armament aid, especially for air warfare, but denounced the pact already two months later, when paving the way for a peace treaty. The first step consisted in a change of president whereby Finland simultaneously freed itself from its commitments to Germany. Elected President of Finland in early August 1944 was the Commander in Chief Mannerheim who had been nominated Marshal of Finland on the 75th celebration of his birthday in 1942.

The 1944 truce which was ratified at the Paris Peace Congress of 1947, returned the borders to the situation in 1940 in Karelia; instead of Hanko the peninsula of Porkkala was now rented to the Soviets for 50 years, and the vast area of Petsamo acquired in 1920 was lost. Finland had to expel the Germans from Lapland, which took several months and caused great devastation. It also had to agree to pay heavy war reparations and accept certain restrictions concerning the size of its army, etc. But the country retained its sovereignty and the Control Committee set up by the allies left the country immediately after the Paris Peace Treaty. The payment of reparations in full in 1952 and the Soviet Union's relinquishment of the Porkkala base in 1955 removed the last restrictions to sovereignty.

The 1941–44 war is known in Finland as the "continuation war" because it was understood as an extension of the Winter War and as an attempt to compensate for losses suffered in that war. The history behind the Winter War explains why Finland participated in the war alongside Germany: in the great power competition between Germany and the Soviet Union/Russia, Finland could not have chosen the side of the Soviet Union in 1941. It was obliged to choose one side or the other for reasons of supplies and in order to avoid a possible occupation like that of Norway and Denmark. But Finnish state leaders and military leaders stressed consistently and with success the special character of Finland and its independence in the war. In Finland there was only very

From Finland's standpoint the enemy in 1939 and 1943 was the same, but those who identified with the western Allies supported Stalin too. Tove Jansson's drawing "The Bolshevik before and now", May 1943, satirizing the Swedish press supporting the Allies.

Finnish territory. The treaty thus came to be a kind of declaration in principle. The Finnish aim to remain outside conflicts between the great powers was mentioned at the beginning of this treaty.

The stabilizing influence of Finland's relations with the Soviet Union was felt in wider circles around the Baltic Sea during the era of Soviet might from the World War until the disintegration of the Union of Soviet Socialist Republics in 1991; from at least the beginning of the 1960's also all the western powers repeatedly recognized the success of Finland's policy of neutrality. Even so, the position of Finland as a good but nevertheless non-socialist neighbour to the Soviet Union was sometimes difficult to perceive both in Finland and the Western countries; when international tension decreased, the position of Finland was admired, during periods of strained relations between the great powers there were doubts about Finnish independence and credibility abroad – not on the part of governments but frequently indeed on that of the press, often on the basis of private Finnish or even more often Swedish views. Every now and then it remained unnoticed that the relationship between Finland and the Soviet Union was built upon the basic geographic factors of the Baltic Sea and the Gulf of Finland region. Soviet security interests and Finland's desire not to become an arena for a conflict between the great powers – to prevent the recurrence of the situation which led to the wars of 1939 and 1941 – remained permanent at

least as long as the Union of Soviet Socialist Republics existed and were fundamentally conveyed to the relationship between Finland and Russia. These military and political viewpoints were in a most essential respect for decades supported by mutual economic interests.

Finland also initiated economic co-operation with the Soviet Union after the war and from 1952 onwards a great share of the products of the war reparation industry became export articles to the Soviet Union.

The period after the war, particularly the period which started in 1952 after the payment of war reparations, resembled the situation at the turn of the century. The Soviet Union's large markets and the Finnish structure of production fit each other well. About 15 to 25% of Finnish exports went to the Soviet Union and for long periods Finland was the Soviet Union's greatest non-socialist trading partner after West Germany. The main import from the Soviet Union was energy; natural gas, nuclear power and above all oil, whereas Finland exported consumer goods such as clothes, shoes and furniture as well as machines and most visibly shipping, ice-breakers and large construction projects, in which the Finns planned and built in the areas of Leningrad, Karelia and Estonia, not only hospitals and hotels but also large harbours and entire industrial towns.

The changeover from barter to foreign exchange trading made Finnish Soviet trade collapse in 1990

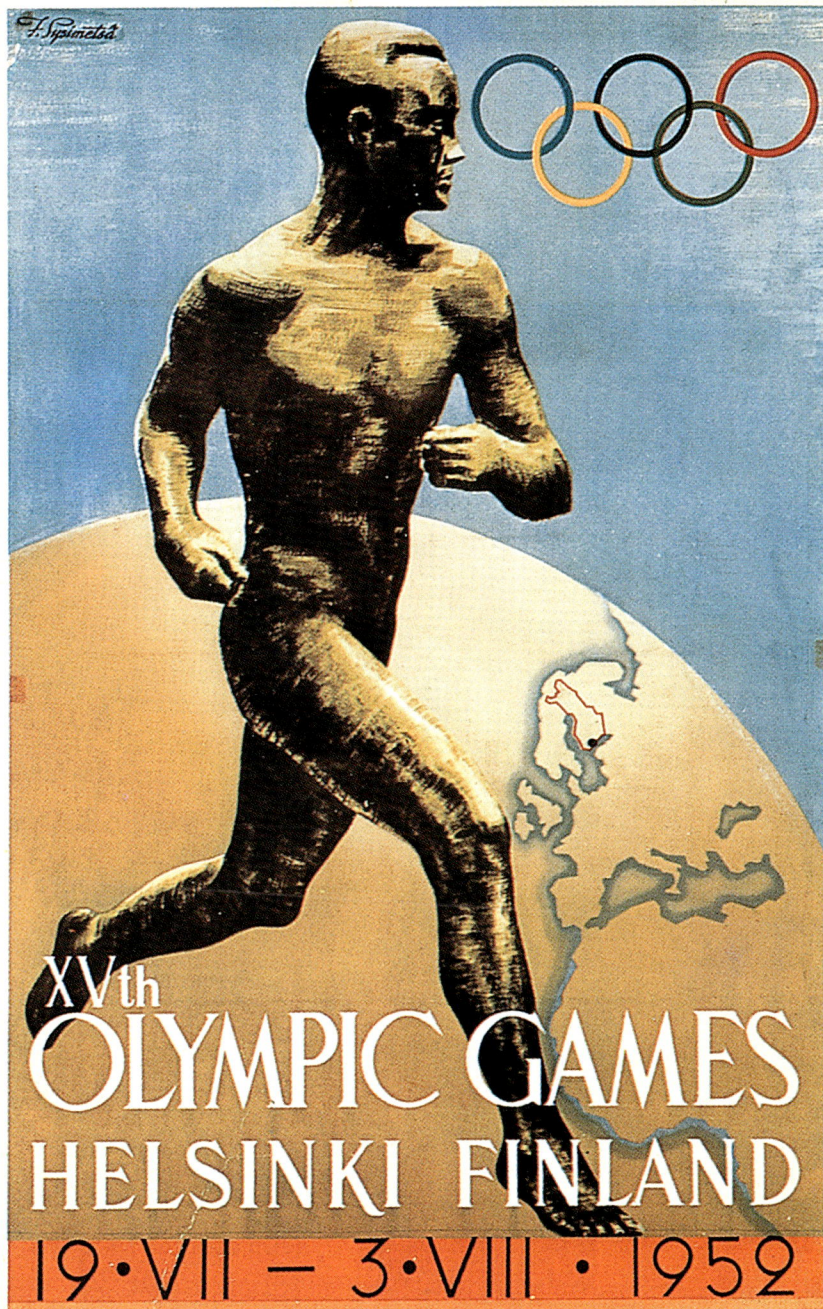

Helsinki had been promised the Olympic Games in 1940 but they were called off because of World War II. The 1952 Olympic Games were held in Finland, although the country was on the losing side in the war. The Games had a very great effect on Finnish self-confidence, and abroad they demonstrated that Finland had survived the war and the postwar period as a western democracy and a nation that had maintained its honour. In the poster the figure of the long-distance runner Paavo Nurmi.

and it was not until 1993 that trade began to slowly recover, but now it was entirely new in structure.

Entering into the great volume of Soviet trade and embarking on long term projects meant a great change in the structure of production immediately after the war. The war reparations demanded by the Soviet Union had to be paid in the form of products defined by the victor, and this forced Finland to speed up its process of industrialization. Commerce between Finland and the Soviet Union made the relationship between the two countries more practical and concrete. Trade thus removed prejudices and those psychological constraints which were brought about by the experiences of war, by the difference in language and culture, and by the differences between socialist societies and market economy democracies. In addition there was still the difference in size between a world power and a small state – in St. Petersburg alone there are about the same number of people as in the whole of Finland. It was of mutual interest to both countries to show that peaceful coexistence between countries of different social systems could function well. Finnish foreign policy led to the fact that at the end of the sixties and during the seventies Helsinki was accepted as neutral territory for important international negotiations in addition to the classical Vienna and Geneva.

Another cornerstone of Finnish post-war politics was the strengthening of co-operation with the other Nordic countries and particularly with Sweden. Es-

pecially after the Baltic countries had been annexed to the Soviet Union and after the economic and cultural impact of Germany in the area of the Baltic Sea had weakened, the Nordic countries – Finland, Sweden, Norway, Denmark and Iceland – drew even closer together. This was expressed by the formation of the Nordic Council, which is an inter-parliamentary body, and many other organs for co-operation particularly in the fields of culture and administration.

The 1960's meant closer economic ties between Finland and Sweden as the movements of the labour force and capital grew quickly, as did trade between the two countries. Finland and Sweden are bound together by innumerable individual and family relationships, cultural ties and a number of joint associations, youth organizations and enterprises. Swedish is still the second national language in Finland and, from the 1960's onwards, every Finnish child has had

During his long term of office President Kekkonen met many world leaders and, with his sharp intelligence, consistent line and stylishness conveyed the message of Finland's independence and enterprise. In the picture the elegant Kekkonen in the Red Square as a guest of the Soviet leaders in 1958.

Stefan: THE HOMES OF THE FINNISH FAMILY

HOME NO. 1:
Rented apartment or condominium
one room + kitchenette, 25 sq.m.

In use 11 months a year

HOME NO. 2:
Cottace: 2 rooms + sauna 30 meters
of beachfront, 2000 sq.m. of forest.

In use 3 weeks to 1 month a year

A key feature of the postwar Finnish identity was a vacation home, with almost every family buying its own summer cottage. The phenomenon reflected the recent migration from the countryside and the thinness of urban tradition. Gradually mass tourism to the Mediterranean area grew alongside and instead of building summer cottages. The caricature compares the restriction of living through the long winter and the relative spaciousness of the short summer season.

to learn its basics at school. After the migration from Finland to Sweden in the 1960's Finnish has had a more prominent position in Sweden. Air traffic and particularly boat traffic between Stockholm and Helsinki and Turku and over the Gulf of Bothnia has increased and thousands of people and dozens or hundreds of lorries are carried over every day.

The mutual relationship between Finland and Sweden as well as between Finland and the other Nordic countries is also expressed in the co-operation between the main political parties. This co-operation reflects the similarity of the Nordic societies and, at the same time, strengthens their cohesion.

Despite the differences, development has gone towards the so-called welfare state in the creation of which the wealthy Sweden, having been spared the war, had a start over the other Nordic countries and in part also acted as an example. The national solidarity in Finland was, however, partly based on other values, particularly on the efforts during and after the war, so that the general trend in Finnish development has been slower and more conservative than that of Sweden. Correspondingly its construction has been based on greater internal unity, which has been expressed at the political level by continuous coalition governments.

The fast urbanization and industrialization of the country during the 1950's created internal tensions not without foreign policy implications, which were brought to the fore in the 1956 presidential election.

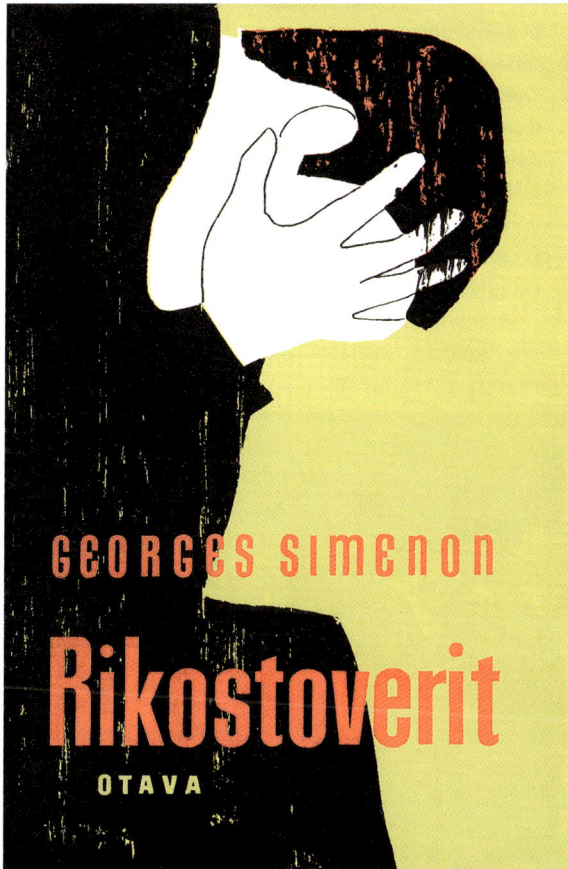

GEORGES SIMENON

Rikostoverit

OTAVA

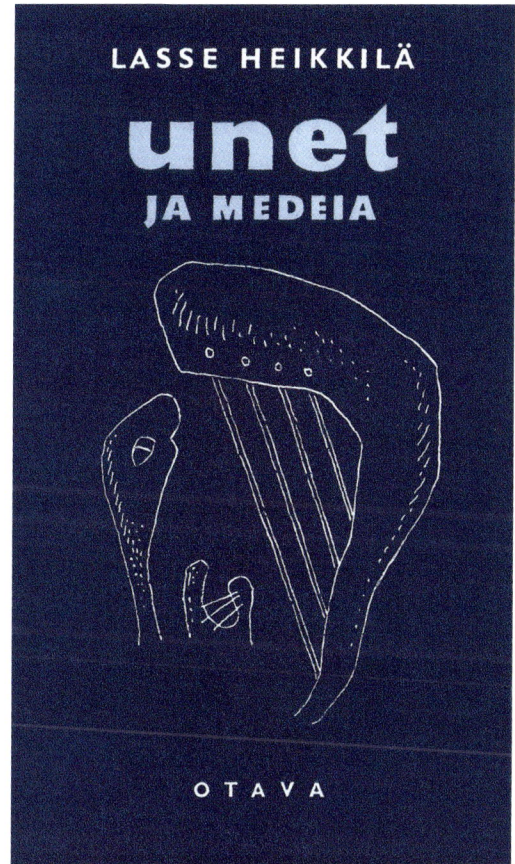

LASSE HEIKKILÄ

unet
JA MEDEIA

OTAVA

Two book covers from the beginning of the 1950s, when much European litera-ture was published in Finnish transla-tion. Many Finnish poets sought inspira-tion from the world of antiquity.

In the electoral college Kekkonen, the candidate for the Agrarian Party won by the smallest possible majority (151–149) over the Social Democrat Fagerholm. In the final stage of the election the former received the support of the People's Democrats and the latter of the Conservatives and Liberals. From the point of view of foreign policy Kekkonen was considered a symbol of the Paasikivi doctrine, whereas Fagerholm was considered the representative of the Nordic-Western doctrine. During Kekkonen's first term of office, first in 1958 with Fagerholm as Prime Minister and later in 1961, Soviet concern over the reflection of great power politics was expressed twice but both times doubts were overcome.

Finland was in fact the only country involved in the second world war which completely fulfilled its obligations to repay the war debt. War reparations had to be paid in the form of industrial goods and this led to a great extent to a change in Finnish industry's production structure and the renewal of machinery. The importance of the metal and engineering industry in particular grew greatly and it developed from a home market industry to an export industry. The traditional export industry, wood processing, expanded and was modernized rapidly, and exports to western countries began soon after the war. In 1961, in order to secure the preconditions of its most important industry, Finland joined EFTA, the European Free Trade Association, and later in 1973 made an extensive customs agreement with the European Economic Community. On both occasions the country was able to secure its economic interests and still emphasize its independence of the political ties of these economic organizations. The agreement with the EEC was followed by a customs agreement with the East European COMECON. The profound political changes in the Soviet Union/Community of Independent States, Germany and the Eastern bloc caused the EFTA-countries to re-negotiate their ties with the European Union in the late 1980's, and early 1990's and subject to popular vote Finland became full member of the EU in 1995.

Postwar economic growth continued until 1974, and Finland profited from this fully, although the immediate postwar years were a difficult time, marked by large investments and the payment of war reparations. Industrial reform was followed from the 1950's on by major infrastructural improvements. The modernization of this large and sparsely-populated country was achieved in a remarkably short time, with such requirements as the construction of a modern road network, electrification, the introduction of regular domestic flights and an extensive programme of housing construction, particularly in towns. This was followed in the 1960's by a phase of rapid development in social security, and in the system of schools and higher education. All these changes served both to increase national prosperity and to reduce social and regional disparities.

Almost all European countries started in the

*Finnish urbanism in the 1960s created large new
residential areas, but the traditional bond with the
forest element was preserved almost everywhere.
Tapiola to the west of Helsinki in 1964.*

1930s to safeguard the lives of poorer citizens through social legislation. The great unemployment and poverty caused by liberalist economic policy around 1930 led to social policy reforms. In countries like Finland the aim was also to fight the pursuit of the social model of Communism and National Socialism. The big need for defence expenditure and then the great financial losses during the war slowed down Finland's development as a welfare state compared with its Nordic neighbours, especially Sweden. The social model of Sweden was an important but dangerous incentive, because Finland's national wealth was less than Sweden's, and the difference became much more pronounced during wartime and the financially difficult period after the war.

The combined Agrarian and Social Democrat government of 1937 put through the first big decisions, maternity benefits for the poor and a general pensions law. The national pensions scheme came into force in 1939, still modest indeed, and in the same year a law was passed concerning paid annual holidays for workers.

Many reforms in the 1940s aimed at helping mothers, children and living ("home establishment loans"). Very important for national health was the municipal maternal and children's clinics system established in 1944, as was the child benefit system implemented in 1948 and covering all children under 16 years of age. State-supported production of dwellings (the Arava loan system) was started in 1949.

The ten years' period 1956-1966 first brought in national pensions for all who had reached the age of 65, then a general workers' pension law (TeL) and in 1964 general health insurance and a 54-day maternity benefit; in 1965 a 40-hour working week was established, which meant free Saturdays for the majority of workers. At the beginning of the seventies came municipal health centres and a municipal child daycare system. At the same time taxes rose, the progressive state income tax and the fixed local taxes, and indirect taxes – the previously small purchase tax – went up.

The oil crisis slump of the 1970s prevented the expanding of social security for over ten years, and measures after that were directed towards supporting children's home care and daycare centres. At the beginning of the 1980s financial aid for all students at universities and professional colleges was raised to the level of some kind of monthly salary. The heavy debts incurred by students ended here. Study in itself has always been free in Finland.

A very big reform was enacted in 1984: the unemployment security system, formerly tied to earnings. It was largely responsible for upsetting the finances of the state and local authorities in the early 1990s, when there was severe unemployment, and contributed to the heavy national debt, but it did save many Finns from distress and poverty.

When the economy showed a strong recovery in the later 1990s, the national debt and persistent un-

"CONTRAPUNCTUS"

Sam Vanni became a conspicuous name in the abstract art of the 1950s and 1960s; he was given the rare title of Academician. In the late 1960s abstract art was, however, rejected, and very loud voices insisted that art should participate directly in social debate. Contrapunctus (1959).

employment still prevented new reforms at a high level. At the same time it had to be accepted that state and local authority social security ("the welfare state") could not be expanded significantly, because the level of taxation had to be lowered to maintain competitive ability and within the framework of the general economic policy of the European Union. With the business cycle weakening again in 2002–2003, the maintaining of the welfare state proved a heavy burden both in Finland and in the whole of Europe. The implementation of the savings demanded by the situation naturally caused dissatisfaction. At the same time it was generally admitted that the recessions taught the importance of ensuring the dynamism of the business world, although this meant that work could not be found for large numbers of unemployed persons.

While Finland in the 1930's was still a very agrarian country, its great period of urbanization and industrialization was late compared to that of many other countries and was correspondingly rather fast. This was naturally reflected in political life as well as in the development of attitudes and ideologies. The housing and placing in productive life of the Karelians and those returning from the front was to be confronted immediately after the war. As the towns and industry could not yet employ all this group, a great number of them were settled in smallholdings, but these proved to be of little worth and played their part in the new great period of migration in the 1960's. Despite the efforts of the Agrarian and People's Democratic Parties in particular to improve the standard of living in the poor areas of eastern and northern Finland, life could not be improved there without big agricultural subsidies.

When, after the 1966 election, the Social Democrats became the leading government party, the rationalization of agriculture was carried out. This meant putting an end to particularly unprofitable smallholdings in northern Finland. The consequence was great migration to the towns of southern Finland and to Sweden, whose expanding industry at that time needed a great deal of manpower. Understandably this "great migration" caused a lot of social problems and was also reflected very noticeably in Finnish literature. The vigorous and popular literary genre of novels and epic literature concentrated for a long time on describing the mental impact of this period of change.

The competition between towns and rural areas, consumers and producers, industry and agriculture governed Finnish post-war politics for a long time, a fact that has not been without foreign policy implications either. As real as competition, however, was the fact that the Social Democrats and the Agrarians had been together in the government most of the time, never on their own it is true, but always as if softened by the inclusion of smaller parties. The authority and often concrete political leadership of the President of the Republic while Kekkonen and Koivisto were in

The products of the Marimek-ko firm, favouring colour and geometrical patterns, became a Finnish symbol for dressing "youngish" urban people. They emphasized the similarity of the sexes and the dominance of "leisure" and informality, a breakaway from the classical European style.

Tapio Wirkkala won international fame at the beginning of the 1950s in Italian design competitions and in the design press. He and other Finns working in glass and wood stressed the originality and archaic quality of the material, a Northern simplicity that attracted continental Europeans who felt they were too much under the pressure of their history. The Italians, moreover, felt a certain need to help the Finns who were on the same losing side in the war.

office had been a very real part of the politics of compromise within the government, as was the constitutional statutory majority regulations which demanded a 2/3 or even 5/6 majority in parliament for the most important bills. The coalitions were often different at the level of local politics. The conservative National Coalition Party was, with the exception of two short periods, in opposition at the national level till 1987 but was at the local level and particularly in larger towns a dominant party and often in coalition with the Social Democrats.

After the first post-war (1945) election the People's Democrats, which gained great popularity, took part in government together with the Agrarians and Social Democrats. This was of great significance during the period of major changes; the participation of the People's Democrats in the government brought many advantages to the workers but at the same time prevented extensive strikes and demonstrations. In 1948, after the events in Czechoslovakia, President Paasikivi nominated a Social Democrat minority government led by Fagerholm. This government lasted for about two years despite the suspicions of the Soviet Union, and was followed by a number of coalition governments led by Urho Kekkonen as Prime Minister, in which the Agrarians were the leading party. When, in 1956, Kekkonen became President he, in turn, nominated his competitor Fagerholm as Prime Minister, but this government came up against internal difficulties, mainly caused by the

Soviet Union's suspicions during the stifling Cold War. After the Soviet Union had stopped trade and called their Ambassador home, the coalition government broke up and the Social Democratic Party split into two for a long time. Only after the 1966 election did the re-united Social Democrats become the leading government party, and in addition to the Agrarians the People's Democrats too were in the government. This reflected President Kekkonen's striving for national unification which, during the period of social changes, was as important as immediately after the war. The Communists, however, did not remain in the government for long and during the 1970's their periods in the government compared to the Social Democrats and Agrarians were short. At the beginning of the 1980's support for the Communist Party declined rapidly.

At the end of the 1960's a new protest party came into being alongside the People's Democrats. The smallholders' or Rural Party (Vennamo), representing the outlying districts of eastern Finland, even became a government party in the 1980's. The longest-standing small party in the government has been the Swedish Party, but the Liberal Party, which was often a government party in the 1950's and 1960's, was faced with a crisis in the 1970's and withered away during the 1980's. The opposition had generally comprised the People's Democrats-Communists on the one hand and the National Coalition Party on the other. The Finnish government had thus been one of the

Finland provided notable assistance in the détente process of the great powers in the 1980s. Finland and its president M. Koivisto enjoyed the confidence of the leaders of both the superpowers. In the picture Presidents Bush and Gorbatchev, with their wives, as guests of President Koivisto and his wife, in September 1990 in the President's Palace where consultations took place. Koivisto impressed Bush with his knowledge of conditions in the Soviet Union, and also influenced the USA to give financial aid to the Soviet. The USA needed Soviet approbation of its Iraq policy, which led to war after a few months. Later in Helsinki at the President's Palace President Ahtisaari also engineered vitally important negotiations concerning the ending of the Bosnian war.

centre-left with the balance changing at times. This long phase ended with a new kind of coalition government from 1987 onward.

After the parliamentary election in 1987, President Koivisto brought the National Coalition Party, which for a long time had been in opposition, into the Government. Harri Holkeri of the National Coalition Party formed a coalition cabinet which conformed to the conventional pattern, except for the fact that the main non-socialist party this time was the National Coalition Party instead of the Centre Party. The Government engaged in the realization of privatization and tax reform following the example of other countries, but the release of foreign exchange trading together with the upswing in trade conditions caused also in Finland as elsewhere a phase of economic overheat and a so-called "casino economy", and the Government was unable to achieve its aim to keep the structural change "under control".

The advantage of the coalition governments has been the ensuring of social stability, and wide representation of different groups of society, the weakness has been group interests and lack of long-term planning. At some stages this appeared in the form of rapid inflation and noisy political dispute, and overemphasis on personalities. Government by coalition, in the period after the oil crisis of 1973, became under the leadership of President Kekkonen and during the long Social Democrat government under Prime Minister Sorsa, government by consensus. The social structures stabilized after the big migration and youth unrest, and under the external pressure of the price development of energy Finland moved into a new kind of successful economic policy. Its aim was, by supporting industry and its competitiveness, to maintain employment and economic growth. Thus the modernization of production carried out in Finland largely under the leadership of the left was completed earlier and more successfully than in most European countries and was based on a broad mutual national understanding.

Finland as most European market economy countries experienced in the late 1980's a period of economic boom associated with a wave of speculation. Finland managed for a long time to preserve the high value of its currency the mark and increased its prosperity with regard to its neighbouring countries as well. The foreign indebtedness of Finland remained for a long time lower than that of many other countries, and the national debt could be reduced. The private sector committed itself more than ever to the international world by means of its proprietary and debt relationships. The technological modernization of industry and many other sectors maintained the international competitiveness of Finland but, on the other hand, the national economy of Finland began through the influence of integration forces to appear rather low. During the period 1990–1991, however, development turned into a decline in Europe as a whole, and this reflected very considerably on Finland, dependent on its export revenues. The shipbuilding industry, which had been successful for a long time, ran into difficulties, and Finland's dependency on the wood processing industry and the engineering industry relative to wood processing was again accentuated. Associated with this was the uncertainty about the preservation of natural resources, emphasized by the growing environmental consciousness of the 1980's. Finland's dependency on the outside world also in terms of environmental inconveniences has often become evident. The military risk effect of e.g. Leningrad-St. Petersburg and the Kola Peninsula regions had to make room in the minds of the Finns for the danger to the environment.

The positive economic development from the end of the 1970's has also had great significance as far as the external esteem of the country is concerned. Finland's policy of neutrality and its position in the world has not always been easily understood abroad. Extensive and successful state visits by President Kekkonen made Finland's position and aims widely known; at the same time extensive cultural and economic co-operation with other countries brought a lot of visitors to Finland to see the country and its circumstances with their own eyes. Kekkonen was able to see the result of his work when Finland received as guests the heads of state and heads of government of 35 countries who signed the Helsinki agreement in 1975 at the final stage of the European

Conference on Security and Co-operation in Europe.

President Kekkonen was re-elected to office in 1962, in 1968, in 1974 and in 1978. In addition to his own Agrarian Party he gained support first from the left and then from the right and finally from almost everybody. After he had fallen ill in 1981 (he died in 1986), the Social Democrat Prime Minister, Mauno Koivisto, was elected President in 1982. In addition to his own party he was supported by some of the People's Democrats and many non-socialist supporters and was elected to office by a greater majority than any previous President under normal circumstances. The tradition of coalition government between the Social Democrats, the Agrarians and the small parties continued till 1987, when the National Coalition Party and the Social Democrats formed a coalition government with Harri Holkeri as Prime Minister. President Koivisto was elected for a new term of office in 1988.

President Koivisto took up where his predecessor had left by engaging in active official state visit policy, and was able to contribute to the process of the leaders of the Soviet Union and the United States approaching each other in the late 1980's. Thus, e.g. the negotiations, during which President Bush and President Gorbachev in 1990 agreed on a mutual policy to pursue in respect of the war against Iraq, which broke out the next year, were held in Helsinki and hosted by President Koivisto. President Koivisto acted in conformity with the Constitution Act as leader

The big age classes and the big social changes were also seen in Finnish street demonstrations. These were connected with domestic strikes and problems, but from the beginning of the 1960's more and more with world politics.

Mika Waltari is the best-known Finnish writer outside his own country with his "Sinuhe the Egyptian" and many other books. In Finland he represented Europeanism and cautious humanism with his historical novels – also his works were in contrast to Finnish rural realism. The Southern Finland Students' Association had a monument raised to his memory in 1985, in the Töölö part of Helsinki. The sculpture, by Veikko Hirvimäki, aroused debate among those in favour of a statue resembling the subject.

in charge of Finnish foreign policy, and the period of international transition, which had begun in 1989, emphasized this task.

In Finland as elsewhere the post-war great age groups went to school in the 1950's and to universities and other institutes of higher education at the end of the 1960's. The ideological and moral change of the age was strongly felt, as was the above-mentioned wave of urbanization which took place at the same time. In university politics a great decentralization programme had already been initiated which was far-reaching in Finland and was followed by a strict *numerus clausus*-policy. The period of political consensus has corresponded to peaceful academic and cultural life in which society has favoured above all "useful" and applied teaching and research. Demands have been made, however, on behalf of more ideological debate and criticism, and since the 1980's Finnish cultural life has once again begun to orientate itself towards its roots in classical Europe. The development of Europe and Finland in the 1990's accentuated these orientations rapidly.

The Holkeri Coalition Cabinet was dissolved as a consequence of the parliamentary election in the spring 1991, and a new government was formed on the basis of the election winners, the Centre Party and the National Coalition Party, with the support of the Swedish People's Party and the Finnish Christian League. Esko Aho, the 36-year old Chairman of the Centre Party, was nominated Prime Minister. Due to the difficulty of the economic situation, the Minister of Finance, Iiro Viinanen, the most important cabinet member of the National Coalition Party, gained a very prominent position as well. Despite Finland's relative prosperity and success during this period, Finns bore in mind the lessons of the war and hard times, resorting to a certain "national egotism".

Postwar life in Finland conformed for a long time to the basic configuration that Finland in terms of its cultural nature, its social system and the major part of its foreign trade belonged to the Nordic countries and the "Western" or "market economy" countries while it was making particular efforts to maintain its good political and trade relations with the Soviet Union. It was supporting and promoting all attempts to relieve tension between the superpowers and strengthen the independence of small nations. On its own part, it emphasized the significance of its own national culture and economy, its active foreign policy and efficient defence forces; these important priorities are in Finland generally adopted and supported by all social groups. Like all small countries, however, Finland was sensitive to sudden fluctuations in international politics and economy and, on a long-term basis, to cultural development trends.

Finland enhanced its defensive capability by ordering some sixty super-effective – and expensive – fighter planes in 1992, despite the financial straits in which the government found itself. During the process of disintegration of the Soviet Union, Fin-

The Finnish composer Kaija Saariaho, who lives in Paris, has won great appreciation as an orchestral and opera composer. She is one of many internationally well-known Finnish musicians of her generation.

economic crisis by both the government and a wide range of non-governmental organizations. After the Soviet Union had ceased to exist as a political entity, President Koivisto in 1991 unilaterally declared the 1948 Treaty on Friendship, Cooperation and Mutual Assistance to have lapsed.

By the latter half of the 1990's, Estonia and Russia had become significant economic players from the Finnish point of view. Trade with Russia, which had petered out to a mere trickle in the interim years, began to revive rapidly, although the new trade was set up on a completely different basis than the previous centralized system. A particularly important component in this new trade consisted of sales by Finnish consumer goods outlets and department stores to Russian private citizens, while the general focus in Finnish-Russian trade shifted to the St. Petersburg region.

The period between 1989 and 1993 was strongly influenced by the dramatic change undergone by the Soviet Union, the Warsaw Pact Countries and Germany.

In 1994, the Treaties of Accession to the EU negotiated by the governments of the new applicants were submitted to approval by referendum. Of the EEA countries, Switzerland and Norway opted to remain outside the Union, whereas the people of Austria, Finland (with a 57% majority) and Sweden (with a 52% majority) voted in favour of accession. Some Finns had misgivings about EU membership

land avoided abrasive foreign policy statements on the Baltic countries, stressing that it could not offer security guarantees to its neighbours, which were gaining their independence at the time. To this extent, official Finnish policy differed from the more rhetorical approach of the Swedish and Danish governments. All the more important, Finland reinforced its cultural ties with Estonia, in particular. Humanitarian aid was provided in the midst of the

Research and its utilization in medicine and agriculture and forestry are new, strong fields in Finland. They are based on very firm academic tradition, and the state has financed innovation to a significant degree. Right from the beginning of the 20th century Helsinki University has had a department of agriculture and forestry, and the Bio Centre seen here was built at the beginning of the third millennium on the Viikki university campus. Finland had already then been a member of the EU for a long time, but Union flags have only gradually become common, because the national flag has been so highly thought of.

on account of nationalist views or for reasons connected with Finland's policy towards Russia, while supporters tended to place the emphasis on the economic benefits and greater security offered by membership. Presumably a great many Finns were swayed in favour of the EU by their wish to emphasize Finland's position within the general European cultural heritage, fearing a false perception of their country and people if it failed to join the Union. Unlike some Norwegians, even those Finns who opposed membership made no attempt to deny the significance of European civilization or to "scare off" people with the threat of Catholicism.

In the internal affairs of Finland, the change in world order resulted both in modifications in the political world and, more commonly, in cultural changes facilitated by factors inherent in the deep structures of culture. On the political level, President Koivisto transferred the emphases on the president-centred exercise of power towards the Government and the Prime Minister. A new kind of political tradition emerged in the presidential elections of 1994, now held without electors in the form of a direct two-phased election. In the primary elections and the first polling round, the voters disregarded the chairmen of the political parties and the political leaders of long-term influence. Rising to the second round, instead of the candidates of the National Coalition Party and

A condition and result of Germany's reunification was that the European Community could move on to become the European Union, at the Maastricht resolutions in 1992. These were approved in all the member countries except Great Britain and Denmark. The Union agreement came into force in November 1992.

The events in Russia and Germany led in the case of Finland to the termination of the Friendship, Cooperation and Mutual Assistance Treaty. Estonia, Latvia and Lithuania finally became independent in 1991. From Finland's standpoint there was much that was positive and encouraging, but at the same time frightening in the possibility of a civil war in Russia, and also famine and a flood of refugees, or conflict between Russia and Estonia. In this situation, in spite of the recession, Finland made military preparations by buying expensive United States Hornet fighter planes and large quantities of armoured vehicles, artillery and other stocks from the former East Germany.

In 1990 there was at once talk of Finland – and Sweden and Norway – joining the European Community, but in the interim a joint European Community and the left-overs of the EFTA organization was established, ETA, which did not start up until 1994. Finland had then, after long public debate, signed a membership application to the European Community in March 1992, which had just approved the founding of the European Union. Finland thus tried to join the Union, which meant tying itself also to a common monetary and economic union and a common security and possibly defence policy. Discussions in Finland were only about economic matters, but under the surface defence aspects and especially Finnish feeling and awareness of histori-

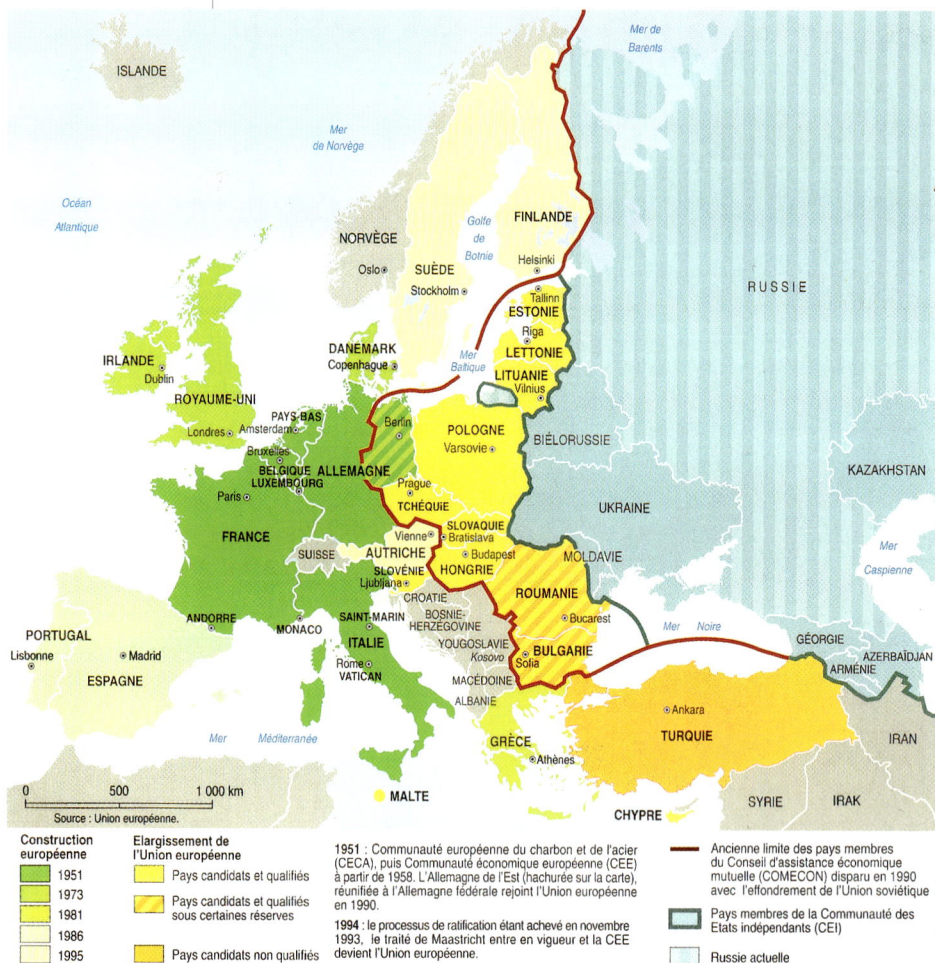

Construction européenne

■	1951
■	1973
	1981
	1986
	1995

Elargissement de l'Union européenne

	Pays candidats et qualifiés
	Pays candidats et qualifiés sous certaines réserves
	Pays candidats non qualifiés

1951 : Communauté européenne du charbon et de l'acier (CECA), puis Communauté économique européenne (CEE) à partir de 1958. L'Allemagne de l'Est (hachurée sur la carte), réunifiée à l'Allemagne fédérale rejoint l'Union européenne en 1990.

1994 : le processus de ratification étant achevé en novembre 1993, le traité de Maastricht entre en vigueur et la CEE devient l'Union européenne.

— Ancienne limite des pays membres du Conseil d'assistance économique mutuelle (COMECON) disparu en 1990 avec l'effondrement de l'Union soviétique

Pays membres de la Communauté des Etats indépendants (CEI)

Russie actuelle

La lente construction européenne

Development of the European Union up to 2002.

cal-cultural belonging to Europe affected the situation.

Negotiations concerning the terms of Finnish membership ended in a favourable agreement for Finland on 1 March 1994, the same day that Martti Ahtisaari took over the Finnish Presidency after the country had been led by Mauno Koivisto for twelve years. Ahtisaari began actively to support a favourable attitude in the referendum concerning entering the Union, which was resolved on 16 October 1994 by a vote of 57% for the Union. Finnish membership came into force at the beginning of 1995, as did those of Austria and Sweden. Those who lost in the referendum accepted the situation surprisingly well. A Norwegian majority, on the other hand, rejected membership. Thus in 1995 the neutral countries between the military alliances, except for Switzerland, joined the EU.

Finland took an enthusiastic and active part in the Union's activities from the start, and won a reputation as a "model pupil", a member who concentrated on important issues and fulfilled its obligations. A logical follow-up was the joining of the economic and monetary union when it was established in 1999, and the transition to a common currency in 2002 – the only Nordic country to do so.

When Finland joined the Union the government was headed by the Centre Party; since 1995 Finland had a five-party coalition government and from 2003 a three-party government. Since there is a majority government and the opposition has been weak, the government has been able to carry on a logical policy supporting the strengthening of the EU.

Finland's successful joining of the EU strengthened its period of Chairmanship of the Union in autumn 1999 – the first new member to hold this office. The prestige accruing to the Chairmanship reinforced Helsinki's status as one of the more conspicuous European cultural capitals at the turn of the century, in the year 2000, the city's 450th anniversary. At the same time Finland had an economic boom and reached the peak of its achievements in technology. The prestige gained and the economic success naturally strengthened Finnish self-confidence and initiative.

The joining of Poland, then the three Baltic countries to NATO changed the Finnish geo-strategic position to some extent. Finland had generally supported the strengthening of the EU and its military defence, but the following of that line slowed down with the United States demanding ever more determinedly worldwide authority, especially after autumn 2001. Finland and Sweden have, however, wished to preserve their neutrality at least for the time being, but still maintain contact with the NATO organization and military material. It has been considered that NATO membership could be expensive and the security guarantees it could offer limited, and that membership of it would draw Finland into world crises without realistic possibility of influencing decision-making.

Joining would weaken Finland's relation with Russia, which is outside NATO. In a crisis between Russia and the United States Finland would not wish to be a theatre of war; if the two countries on the other hand are on good terms with one another, there is no military danger.

Since Norway did not wish to join the EU, and Denmark did not accept the Maastricht decisions, while Sweden did not enter the monetary union, Finland's international position in Northern Europe was emphasized. In addition, this was enhanced by Finland's frontier position as regards Russia and Estonia, and the police and customs obligations caused by this when the Schengen agreement came into force.

In 2002, when the joint monetary currency was adopted, only three of the small Baltic countries of the Finnish Gulf coastal states had the same relation to the EU and to NATO, whereas Russia, Finland, Sweden, Poland and Germany all had a different relation to these international organizations; of these Finland is the representative of the most purely European line. At the end of the year it was decided that Estonia, Latvia, Lithuania and Poland, four other former communist states and two Mediterranean islands should join the Union. Thus the Union gained a more Baltic character.

the Centre Party, was Mrs. Elisabeth Rehn, of the Swedish People's Party, who had won popularity as "the world's first woman Minister of Defence". The winner of the election by an approx. 54 per cent majority was Martti Ahtisaari, candidate of the Social Democrats, Secretary of State of the Ministry for Foreign Affairs, who had never been a member of parliament nor a cabinet minister and had the merits of a significant career in international organizations, particularly in the United Nations, and such loose ties to the Party that he received twice the votes of the general support of the Social Democrats. Brought up in the election debate instead of party politics were topics relative to international affairs, humanity and, surprisingly enough, religion; the principal candidates agreed wholeheartedly about many important issues, particularly on the desirability of Finland joining the European Union.

After the heady economic growth of the '80s, from 1990 on the Finnish economy plunged headlong into a deepening recession. Almost complete deregulation of the money market had resulted in increased borrowing by the government, businesses and private individuals, acting on the assumption of continued growth. The ensuing economic retrenchment made the debt a major public – and private – problem, leaving many major and minor economic players bankrupt, and trapping the entire banking system in a serious crisis. The government came to the rescue by taking over the liabilities of the insol-

vent banks, and was able to prevent many private and business debacles and complete economic chaos at the cost of a growing public debt and a high rate of taxation. Meanwhile, the unemployment rate rose rapidly to nearly 20% of the working-age population. Unemployment brought financial worries and identity problems to many individuals and families, and seriously strained the national economy; nonetheless, Finland held on to the fundamental principles of the welfare state, averting the real pauperization of the jobless.

Among the major reasons for the crisis were the sudden and unexpected halt to trade with the Soviet Union and the excessive debt contracted during the boom years; high unemployment was also caused in part by the high cost of labour, leading to the rapid and effective automation of production. Inflation came virtually to a standstill, as did the mechanism of annual payrises. The Finnish mark had to be allowed to float from 1992 on, but in 1996 it returned – before the currencies of several other Union countries – to a semi-fixed exchange rate within the Union's exchange-rate mechanism. This decision was preceded by the government's declaration of commitment to the objectives of the Maastricht Treaty and to Finland's participation in the first stage of monetary union.

The EU Presidency and the designation of Helsinki as European City of Culture were not the only auspicious events to mark the millennium in Finland. In February 2000, Tarja Halonen – Foreign Minister and candidate of the Social Democratic Party – became the first woman to be elected President of Finland, gaining 53% of the votes in the second round of voting. Halonen and the other main contender Esko Aho (a former Prime Minister from the Centre Party) split the vote both regionally and between men and women. Despite the divisive nature of the electoral system, the general mood of the elections was amicable, reflecting the spirit of consensus prevailing in the coalition government.

To the new Millennium

President Ahtisaari came into office on 1 March 1994. He started actively to encourage a favourable attitude in the coming referendum concerning Finland's entry to the EU, and together with the Prime Minister Esko Aho influenced Finland's joining the Union in the decisive stage. The Social Democrat president and the Centre–Right-wing government together formed a coalition that communicated to the nation that at least almost all the country's political leadership supported joining the Union. It was in fact important for Finland to show that, contrary to many prejudices concerning "Finlandization" that existed abroad, it belonged – historically, culturally and economically, to western Europe. The Finns showed their pro-EU attitude compared with their Nordic neighbour countries by joining the European Economic and Monetary Union in its founding stage, by adopting the Euro currency for exchange accounts in 2000, and Euro notes and coins for normal Finnish use at the beginning of 2002. Alongside this, Finland's prestige was enhanced by President Ahtisaari's very successful activity in settling international crises; in these processes Helsinki could again act as a place for the highest level international diplomacy.

Finland's favourable attitude to the EU has been explained in various ways. Some have seen it primarily as seeking security against Russia, and this thinking has led to stronger proposals to seek membership of the military alliance NATO. Less emphasis has been given to what is perhaps a more important factor, that the Finns themselves have always known that they belong to western Europe as regards culture, legislation, the church and educational system (including language learning). In the economic sphere, Finnish foreign trade at the time of joining the EU was entirely oriented towards the west, with the collapse of the old trade with the Soviet Union.

Perhaps the most important thing, however, is to see the continuity with which Finland right from the late 1950s, from the EFTA debate and the EEC debate 1972–1973, had prepared itself for the development of European unity. In the 1980s Finland joined many European technical and scientific cooperative organizations. The discussion concerning the European Economic Area also smoothed the road to joining the Union. Presidents Kekkonen and Koivisto had represented the "de Gaulle" concept of European independence: the developing of European institutions by trying to relieve the bipolar danger of the world system. Thus they could have got the Soviet Union too, even though unwillingly, to agree to Finland continuing to be tied to the West without commercial or political demonstrations. Joining the Union was logical; remaining outside it would have been illogical and would have equated Finland with those post-Communist countries whose joining the Union in 2004 was confirmed at a series of summit meetings, starting with that in Helsinki in 1999. The final decision was made at the Copenhagen summit meeting in 2002 and signed in Athens in 2003.

President Martti Ahtisaari has a long background in important United Nations tasks, and he gained a significant international reputation during his presidency as an international negotiator and arbitrator. In the picture Martti Ahtisaari surrounded by journalists in Belgrade, June 1999, where he had been negotiating for peace in Kosovo together with Viktor Tchernomyrdin, the former Russian Prime Minister.

Finland's successful adjustment to the Union was vitally affected by the unprecedented stability of Finnish government policy. When the Social Democrats won the election, their leader Paavo Lipponen assembled a big coalition, a "rainbow government", in 1995, which included along with the Prime Minister's party the Right-wing party, the Greens, the Left-wing party and the Swedish party. The breadth of the coalition aroused international attention and surprise, but proved very successful, and the government was re-appointed in 1999. Lipponen's long-lived, broadly-based government had to start off un-der difficult conditions of heavy unemployment and a large national debt, but its broad political coverage prevented significant expressions of discontent, while the Centre Party in opposition could offer few alternatives. The government was rewarded by a continued improvement of the economy, especially the big profits that the Nokia company brought to Finland, and structural reform, but the level of unemployment fell only slowly to around 10%, high by European standards, and not below it.

In 2000 Finland also got a new, or actually its first, comprehensive constitution instead of the

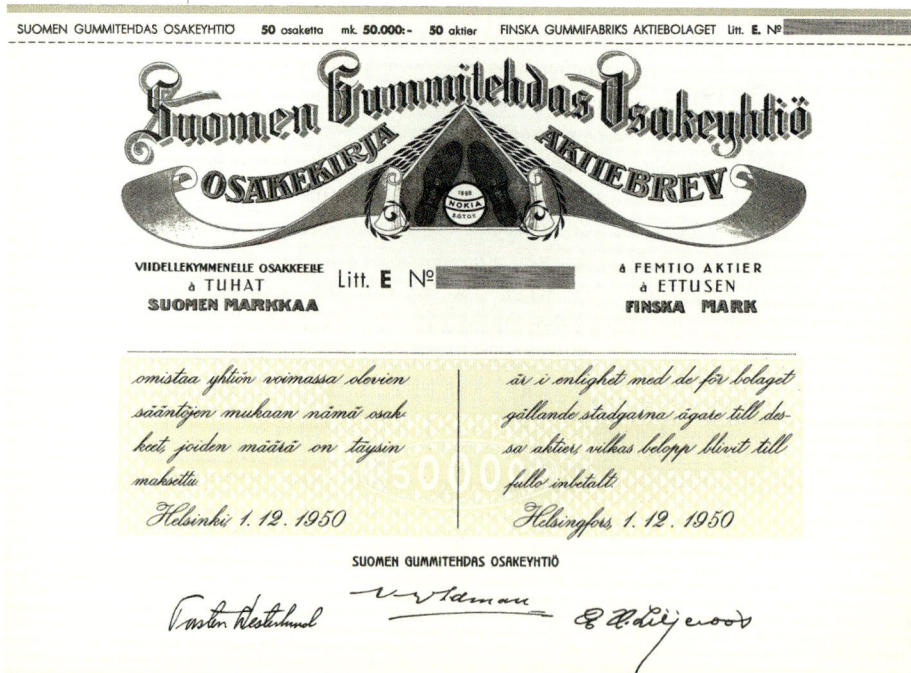

| SUOMEN GUMMITEHDAS OSAKEYHTIÖ | 50 osaketta | mk. 50.000:- | 50 aktier | FINSKA GUMMIFABRIKS AKTIEBOLAGET Litt. E. Nº |

Suomen Gummitehdas Osakeyhtiö

OSAKEKIRJA — AKTIEBREV

VIIDELLEKYMMENELLE OSAKKEELLE
à TUHAT   Litt. **E** Nº   à FEMTIO AKTIER
SUOMEN MARKKAA   à ETTUSEN
FINSKA MARK

omistaa yhtiön voimassa olevien
sääntöjen mukaan nämä osak-
keet, joiden määrä on täysin
maksettu.

Helsinki 1.12.1950

är i enlighet med de för bolaget
gällande stadgarna ägare till des-
sa aktier, vilkas belopp blivit till
fullo inbetalt.

Helsingfors 1.12.1950

SUOMEN GUMMITEHDAS OSAKEYHTIÖ

In the old share certificate of the Finnish Rubber Factory the word Nokia can be seen, surrounded by rubber galoshes.

The Finnish electronics company Nokia became the world's leading manufacturer and developer of the mobile phone from the mid-1990s. Its success vitally affected the Finnish national economy, and at the same time enhanced Finnish self-confidence. The rise of Nokia occurred at the same time as Finland joined the EU and the Euro monetary system, and – the first of the countries that joined in 1995 was given the task of chairing the Union.

Nokia's shares rose extremely rapidly, at an annual rate of 40-60 per cent, and exceeded 30 billion Euros at the turn of the century – the Finnish national budget then was 35 billion Euros (year 2000).

The enormous growth of the Nokia share value made the company a legend – between 1991 and 2001 the value rose 233-fold – and a little earlier shares were sold with a 400-fold profit. In 2002 Nokia's share value, like that of companies generally all over the world, dropped significantly, but Nokia retained its position, profitability and volume, though other enterprises in the field ran into difficulties.

The rise of Nokia was affected by several current features and skilful utilization of them. But there are many important factors in the background of this success. The name of the firm goes back to a pioneer enterprise established in 1865 in the field of mechanical wood processing, which later – in 1967 – merged with a company in the chemical industry, a rubber factory and a firm manufacturing telephones and electric cables. Some of these industrial branches had long depended on the Russian market in Imperial days. When trade with the Soviet Union once more became an important factor in the Finnish economy after World War II, the export of cables there again proved very profitable. Products of the wood processing industry were sold mostly to western countries, and those of the rubber industry to the home market. In this respect Nokia's history throws light on Finnish history: relations with the Soviet Union were important, they were handled skilfully, and they did not prevent orientation towards the west. This became evident later, when the United States tried to prevent the export of technology to the Soviet Union. Nokia then managed with the support of the Finnish state to keep its markets in both West and East.

Nokia's success was also founded on two Finnish factors. First, the Finnish state concentrated funds on product development and research in technology, in cooperation with EUREKA and in other ways. Second, the international economic phenomenon called deregulation – the dissolving of economic regulations – was implemented in Finland in the telecommunication field earlier and more consistently than in many other countries. This was to Nokia's advantage.

The deregulation policy, however, also had the threatening consequence that the Finnish economy suffered a serious crisis, starting in 1990. This was primarily a banking crisis, for the banks had increased their volume enormously when regulation was dissolved and foreign loans could be taken freely, and many firms and private persons had taken large loans. Security for the loans was in estate and dwellings, the value of which quickly fell when the boom turned to a slump. Banks suffered a drastic crisis; the government had to save them to prevent countless citizens and enterprises from going bankrupt. An important background factor was that the Soviet Union plunged into a profound economic and political crisis, a period of extreme depression, which put an almost complete end to Finland's so important trade with Russia for many years.

Nokia was also in trouble for some time, but mobile phones and communications had by now developed commercially to a very profitable level. Nokia's investments in research and development in the field now proved their worth.

Although Nokia's ownership mainly shifted abroad, numerous Finnish companies, foundations and private persons, together with the state, won considerable profits from the rise in value of Nokia shares. Thus Nokia's success influenced the community favourably in many ways, and this in turn spread general optimism, along with the political stability of the coalition, "rainbow" government, and the enthusiasm aroused by participation in the EU. Nokia millionaires were a new object of admiration and envy in the very egalitarian Finland – and the millionaires themselves were quite bewildered.

Nokia's success must be set in the context of certain basic trends in Finland. In a broad international study (PISA) in 2002 Finns were placed in the lead in a comparison of young people's literacy, and among the first in the world as regards the low level of corruption. Thus Finland appeared as a technical, hard-working and honest nation, with a confidence inherited from the wartime as a significant background effect. In the sphere of humanist and artistic culture Finland's old European tradition has not developed so well. Perhaps in the course of time sponsors for art and culture will be found once more.

*Change of president, 2000: the Speaker of the Parlia-
ment, Mrs. Riitta Uosukainen, a teacher of Finnish
in "civil" life, congratulates the new President Mrs.
Tarja Halonen. To the right the retiring President
Martti Ahtisaari. The Presidents are wearing the
emblems of the three State Orders.*

former number of constitutional laws (the most important of these being the form of government of 1919 and the parliamentary system of 1906 with its amendments). Dissenting from the government's proposal, the Parliament changed the focus of formal power by reducing the president's authority, against the attitude of the nation's majority expressed in all opinion polls. No greater actual change in the mutual significance of functions of the state, however, could be observed in the initial years. This was principally because of the broad and long-lived government, and the Prime Minister's strong position. The domination of the Parliament in the new constitution is understandably chiefly only an attitude in principle if and when the country is governed by a large coalition and there is no strong opposition.

The long period of ascendancy of the Lipponen government meant above all the pursuit of a policy of economic dynamism. The stability created by the long, safe work relations of the state and large enterprises changed to a new kind of work atmosphere, as one domestic and foreign merger followed another, and state operations were transferred to privatized firms. The object of the mergers and privatization has been to try to manage with a smaller but more effective work force; therefore unemployment has remained high. The aim of achieving dynamism has been implemented by putting a lot into research, and the teaching system has been "whipped" into efficiency. Alongside the research universities, an extensive system of professional colleges has been established. Helsinki, Tampere and Oulu have shaped dynamic economic development centres, which have succeeded in creating new kinds of jobs in the fields of high tech and innovation.

The tradition of the coalition government was continued after the elections of spring 2003, when the Social Democrats and the Centre Party formed a majority government along with the little Swedish Party, led by the former opposition leader Mrs. Anneli Jäätteenmäki of the Centre Party. The 2003 elections offered an unconcealed view of the Finnish political system. In the electoral campaign the Social Democrats, the leading party in the coalition of that time, were strongly criticized by the Centre party, but nevertheless they formed a coalition government together. Apparently the general opinion was quite satisfied by this traditional decision.

Although Finland's general wealth has increased during boom periods, the country's national wealth is still not great. The example of Finland's rich neighbour Sweden has for its part led to good enterprise and sometimes too early and expensive reforms. The high comparative points awarded to Finland at the beginning of the new millenium for dynamism, low level of corruption, literacy of the young, and in comparative connections have had an encouraging effect. Recessions and international tension have, however, preserved Finland's realization that success is only relative.

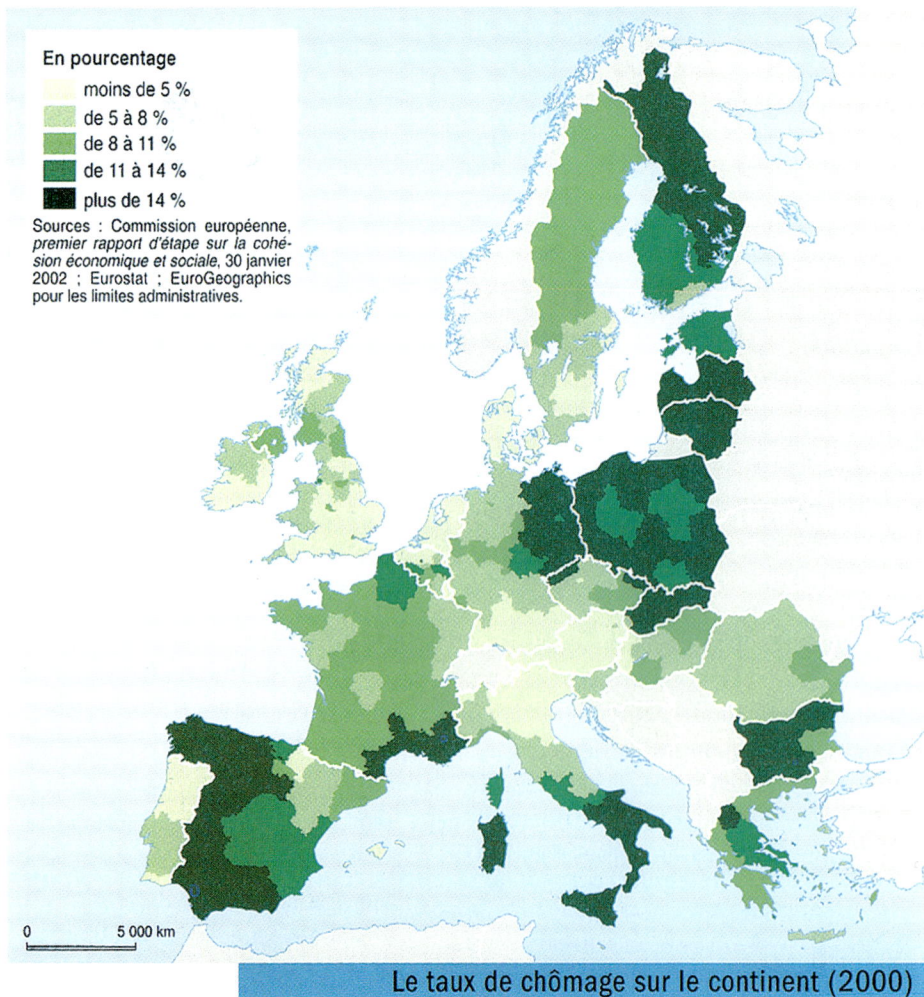

En pourcentage

moins de 5 %
de 5 à 8 %
de 8 à 11 %
de 11 à 14 %
plus de 14 %

Sources : Commission européenne, premier rapport d'étape sur la cohésion économique et sociale, 30 janvier 2002 ; Eurostat ; EuroGeographics pour les limites administratives.

0   5 000 km

Le taux de chômage sur le continent (2000)

Finnish economic development was very favourable, especially from the mid-1990s, but its weak point was the relatively high level of unemployment. This was largely due to the extensive structural reform, which pushed aside less well-trained groups of workers and others, so that it may be reckoned that those with jobs are very well qualified. But Finland has also wished by international standards to take comparatively good care of the unemployed.

In the maps the Finnish situation is pictured unreasonably, because the large sparsely populated area burdened by unemployment covers much space, but the densely populated Southern Finland with a high rate of employment is given little attention. The Helsinki region is part of Europe's wealthy "heartland".

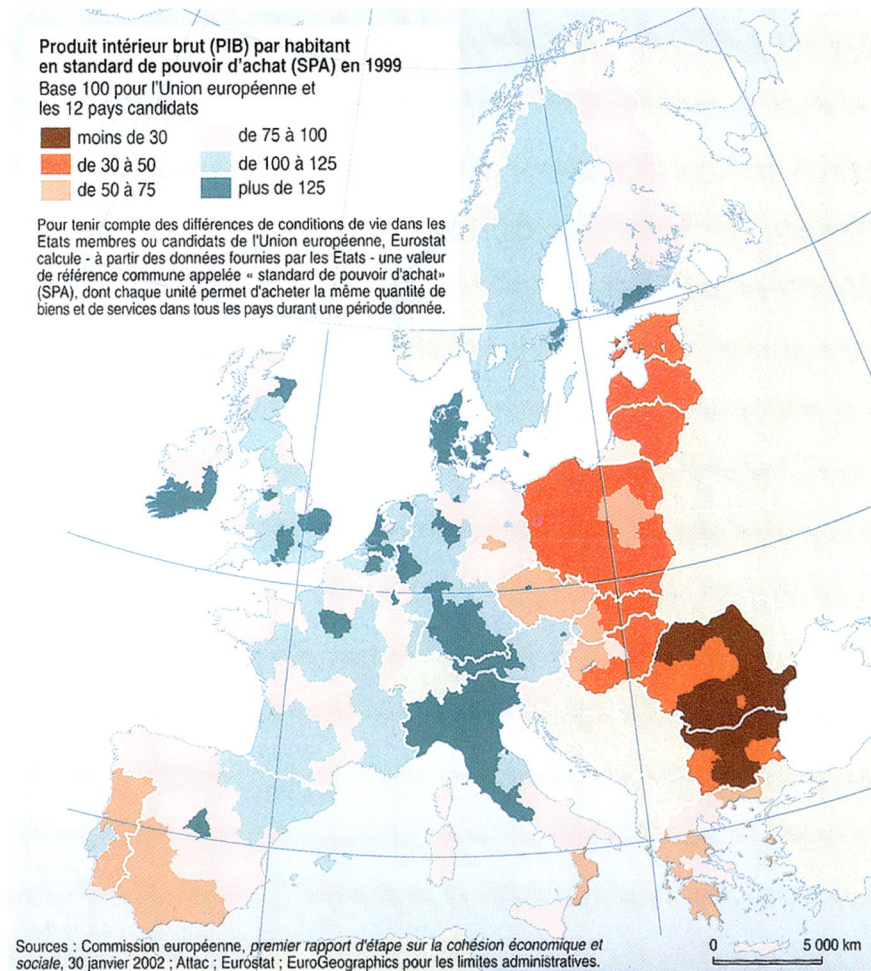

Produit intérieur brut (PIB) par habitant en standard de pouvoir d'achat (SPA) en 1999
Base 100 pour l'Union européenne et les 12 pays candidats

- moins de 30
- de 30 à 50
- de 50 à 75
- de 75 à 100
- de 100 à 125
- plus de 125

Pour tenir compte des différences de conditions de vie dans les Etats membres ou candidats de l'Union européenne, Eurostat calcule - à partir des données fournies par les Etats - une valeur de référence commune appelée « standard de pouvoir d'achat» (SPA), dont chaque unité permet d'acheter la même quantité de biens et de services dans tous les pays durant une période donnée.

Sources : Commission européenne, *premier rapport d'étape sur la cohésion économique et sociale*, 30 janvier 2002 ; Attac ; Eurostat ; EuroGeographics pour les limites administratives.

0   5 000 km

Cœur prospère, marges pauvres

The position of Finland on the periphery of Europe, but nevertheless close to its important borders and in the sphere of various influences, has compelled Finland to delve into history, to find there the continuity of settlement and production, on the one hand, and the influence of great changes in world politics, on the other hand, and to assess its own ability to meet these time-imposed challenges. The tradition of the Swedish rule lies deep in the structure of Finland, its social system and world of concepts. The tradition of the Grand Duchy era and subsequent relations with Russia stays alive in the sense that the Finns have a way of thinking internationally and realistically. Inherent in the republic's tradition are the perseverance and spirit of self-sacrifice displayed in times of war and difficulties, and the sense of solidarity in a tight spot.

The many changes and crises Finland has gone through in the past have equipped us with the capacity to find new solutions and adjust to new situations in world politics. At the same time, Finns are as aware as ever today of the importance of fostering the social, moral and cultural values implicit in the common European heritage. All these features may, however, well be considered to constitute parts of the general European social and moral culture, to which Finland has belonged for almost a millennium.

The 1990's were the first decade of considerable immigration, and Finland learned to live with members of nations who had come from far places. But the largest group of immigrants came from nearby Russia.
Large immigrant movements had previously been seen after the Russian Revolution and when the Karelians were settled in Finland after the wars in 1940 and 1944.

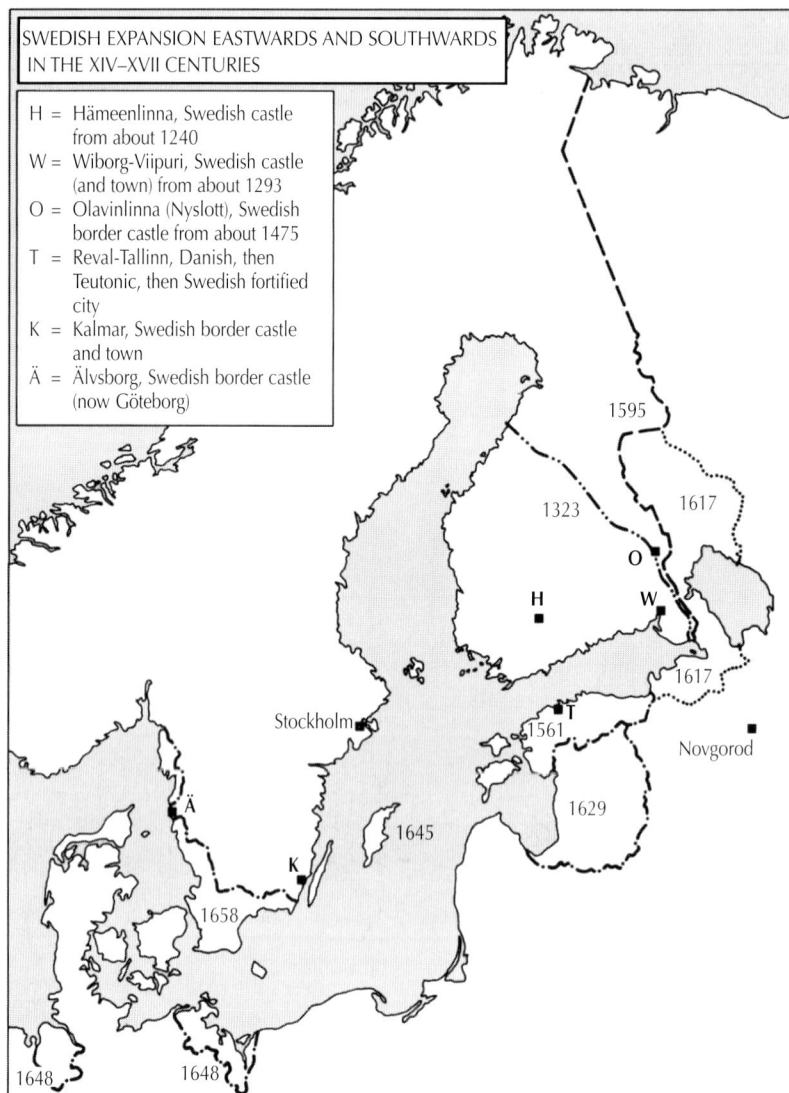

SWEDISH EXPANSION EASTWARDS AND SOUTHWARDS
IN THE XIV–XVII CENTURIES

H = Hämeenlinna, Swedish castle
from about 1240
W = Wiborg-Viipuri, Swedish castle
(and town) from about 1293
O = Olavinlinna (Nyslott), Swedish
border castle from about 1475
T = Reval-Tallinn, Danish, then
Teutonic, then Swedish fortified
city
K = Kalmar, Swedish border castle
and town
Ä = Älvsborg, Swedish border castle
(now Göteborg)

RUSSIAN EXPANSION WESTWARDS IN THE XVIII–XIV CENTURIES

B = Bomarssund, Russian (-Finnish) fortress, built in the 1830's. Destroyed in the Crimean War.
H = Hamina (Fredrikshamn), Swedish, then Russian Fortress, built in the 1720's.
K = Kronstadt, Russian Fortress
S = Sveaborg (Suomenlinna), by Helsinki. Built 1748 as Swedish fortress; Russian fortress 1809–1918.

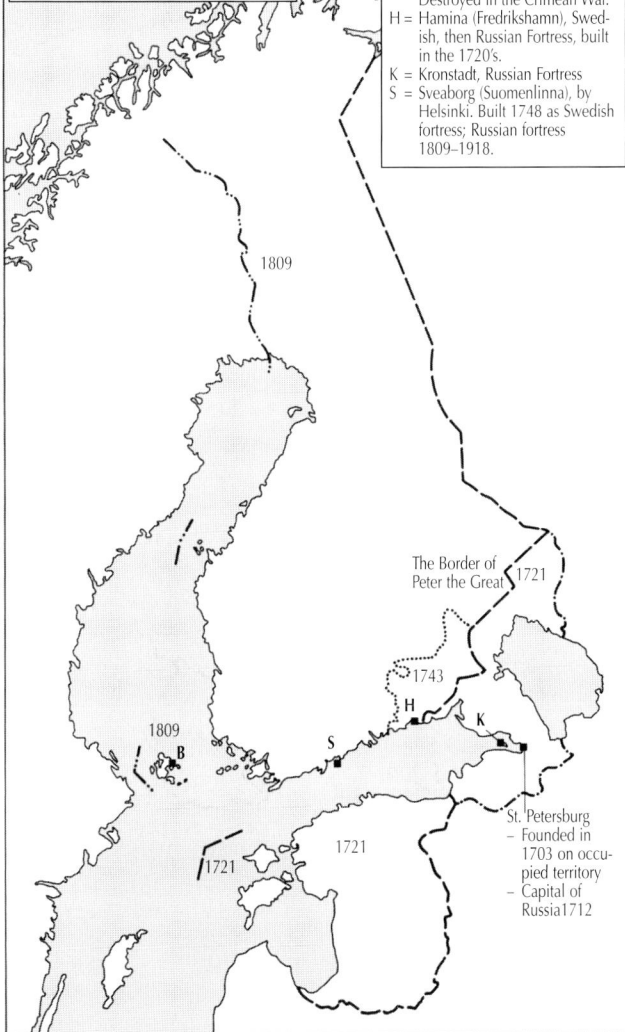

1809

The Border of Peter the Great 1721

1743

H

K

S

1809

B

1721

1721

St. Petersburg
– Founded in 1703 on occupied territory
– Capital of Russia 1712

FINLAND'S AND ESTONIA'S BORDERS IN THE XX CENTURY

H = Hanko-Hangö (Soviet 1940–41)
P = Porkkala (Soviet 1944–56)

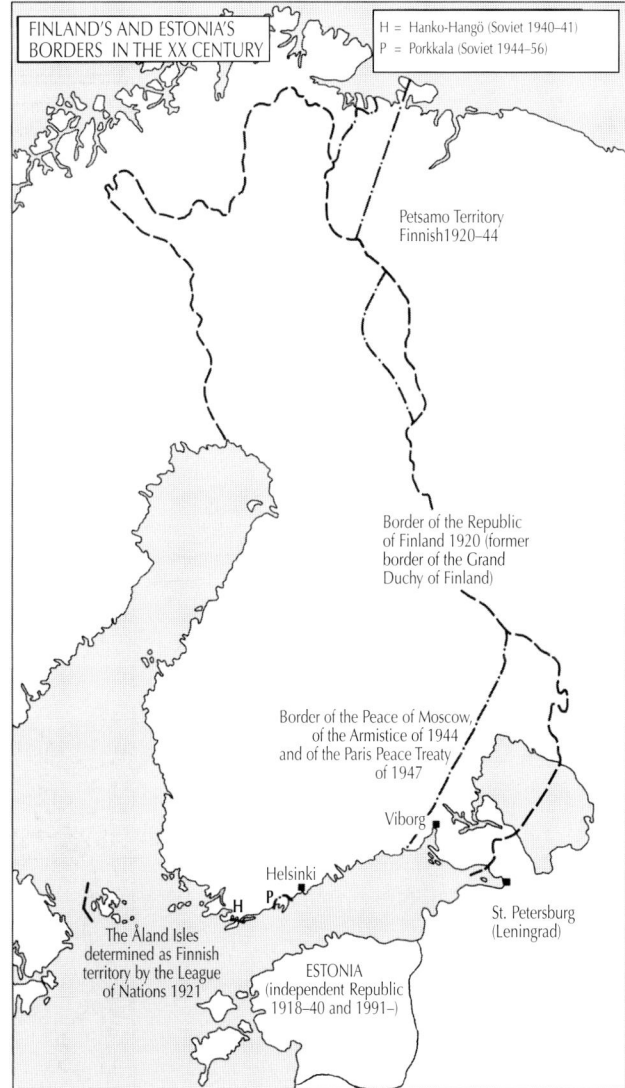

Petsamo Territory Finnish 1920–44

Border of the Republic of Finland 1920 (former border of the Grand Duchy of Finland)

Border of the Peace of Moscow, of the Armistice of 1944 and of the Paris Peace Treaty of 1947

Viborg

Helsinki

P

H

The Åland Isles determined as Finnish territory by the League of Nations 1921

ESTONIA (independent Republic 1918–40 and 1991–)

St. Petersburg (Leningrad)

PHOTOGRAPHS

O

TAVA ARCHIVES

7, 10, 11, 26, 27, 29–34, 39, 40, 43, 48, 50, 51, 52/ István Ràcz, 12/ Matti Huuhka, 13, 15 left, 17, 19, 21,
25 below / N. Naumoff, 61–63, 67–69, 71, 72, 79, 83–88, 93, 100–106, 108, 109, 111–113, 115, 116,
117/ Jussi Aalto, 119, 125, 127/ Finnish Army, 129, 137, 141, 145, 147, 149, 150 left, 158, 159

DEPARTMENT OF MUSEUMS 35/ P-O Welin, 44/ Museokuva, 60, 75, 89, 90, 95 below/ Jussi Aalto
EERO ROINE 38
FINNISH ARMY 121, 123
FINNISH NATIONAL GALLERY 14 below, 54, 70, 118/ Hannu Aaltonen, 59/ Jukka Romu
FINNISH NATIONAL MUSEUM 77, 82, 97
HACKMAN DESIGNOR LTD. 150 right.
HELSINKI CITY MUSEUM 64/ Jan Alanco, 156
HELSINKI UNIVERSITY LIBRARY/ AV center 49, 65
HELSINKI UNIVERSITY MUSEUM 55
LEHTIKUVA 21/ Kimmo Mäntylä, 132, 139/ Kalle Kultala, 152/ Jaakko Avikainen, 155/ Heikki Saukkomaa,
158/ Heikki Kotilainen, 159/ Martti Kainulainen, 165/ Kimmo Mäntylä, 168, 173/ Jussi Nukari
LIISA SUVIKUMPU 6, 25 above, 95 above, 166
MATTI KLINGES ARCHIVES 9, 14 above, 15 right, 16, 20, 37, 41, 42, 46, 56, 66, 74, 80, 91, 92, 94, 96–99, 110,
120, 126, 130, 142, 160, 170, 171
O. A. MANKELL 76
REGIONAL COUNCIL OF SOUTHWEST FINLAND / P-O Welin 18, 22–24
STEFAN / Tapani Kovanen 140
WAR ARCHIVES, STOCKHOLM 58